MEN-AT-ARMS SE

EDITOR: MARTIN WINDROW

The Indian Mutiny

Text by
CHRISTOPHER
WILKINSON-LATHAM

Colour plates by
G. A. EMBLETON

OSPREY PUBLISHING LONDON

Published in 1977 by
Osprey Publishing Ltd
12–14 Long Acre, London WC2E 9LP
Member Company of the George Philip Group

ISBN 0 85045 259 7

Filmset by BAS Printers Limited, Wallop, Hampshire
Printed in Hong Kong

The author would like to acknowledge the extensive use he
has made of the following books: N. A. Chick (ed.), *Annals
of the Indian Rebellion 1857–58* (London, 1859/60), C. J.
Griffiths, *The Siege of Delhi* (London, 1910) and also the diary
of H. D. Bishop. The photographs are by courtesy of the
National Army Museum, except for nos. 14, 19, 23, 24.

The Devil's Wind

'I know not what course events may take. I hope they may not reach the extremity of war. I wish for a peaceful time of office, but I cannot forget that, in our Indian Empire, the greatest of all blessings depends upon a greater variety of chances and a more precarious tenure than in any other quarter of the globe. We must not forget that in the sky of India, serene as it is, a small cloud may arise, at first no bigger than a man's hand, but which growing bigger and bigger, may at last threaten to overwhelm us with ruin.' These words, spoken by Lord Canning at a banquet given in his honour by the Directors of the Honourable East India Company, on 1 August 1855, were tragically prophetic, for within two years the 'Devil's Wind' swept across the Bengal Presidency threatening the end of British rule in the jewel of the Empire.

At the time of the Mutiny there were many views as to its origin; one was that it was a widespread conspiracy, carefully organized for the overthrow of British power in India, and another that it was merely a military rising. The men with the best opportunity of judging came to diametrically opposed conclusions. Sir John Laird Muir Lawrence, KCB, Chief Commissioner of the Punjab, held the opinion that the mutiny had its origin in the army and that its final cause was the 'cartridge affair' and nothing else. Sir James Outram, the Chief Commissioner for Oudh, with the supreme command of the troops in that province, believed that it was the result of a Mohammedan conspiracy making capital out of Hindu grievances and that the cartridge affair merely precipitated the Mutiny before it had been organized into a popular insurrection. Brigadier John Nicholson, CB, stated that in his view, 'Neither greased cartridges, the annexation of Oudh, nor the paucity of European officers were the causes. For years I have watched the army and felt sure they only wanted their opportunity to try their strength with us.'

Whichever appraisal was accepted at the time, the basic origins of the revolt of the Bengal Army lay in the reaction of the conservative section of the Indian population to the modernizations introduced by the British, and the complete lack of knowledge about and sympathy with the people

1. **Lord Canning, Governor-General of India during the Mutiny.**

3

2. **Bahadur Shah, last of the Mughal Emperors of India.**

invading the realms of both faith and caste and a widespread belief was held that Lord Canning (Governor-General 1856–62), Dalhousie's successor, had been sent to India with the brief to convert the country to Christianity. It was unfortunate that the essayist Macaulay, at one time a member of the Governor-General's Council, had, in his writings, disparaged Hindu mythology. *Suttee*, the custom whereby a Hindu widow sacrificed herself on her husband's funeral pyre, and infanticide had been abolished as cruel and barbaric. Western science, astronomy and surgery were all opposed to the teachings of the Brahmins and the telegraph and railways were looked upon as magical and devilish works of the British. Sir William Lee-Warner, in his *Life of the Marquess of Dalhousie* said that, 'Even the most ignorant and apathetic Hindu was brought into more conscious touch with the spirit of the West during the eight years preceding 1857 than at any other period in the history of India.'

From the military standpoint the balance of European and Indian troops in India had been seriously affected by the Crimean War. By 1857 the native element in the army had reached the enormous number of 233,000 men and outnumbered the Europeans and the Queen's troops by nearly seven to one. There was also a serious deficiency of officers of the best type, needed in administrative posts on the frontier; and in addition to this the distribution of the army was bad, the great centres of Delhi and Allahabad being garrisoned entirely by native troops and there being only one British regiment (at Dinapoor) between Allahabad and Calcutta.

High caste sepoys in the Bengal army, the Brahmins and Rajputs, would lose their caste if they served out of India. In the past their reluctance to do so had been respected, but in July 1856 the General Service Enlistment Act was passed, which forbade the enlistment of any man not willing to serve wherever he was required, even overseas if necessary. Great uneasiness was caused by this reform for it meant that all high-caste men who wanted to join the army would either have to renounce their caste or forego their chosen career.

The story of the greased cartridges, although well known, must be repeated. Late in 1856 the

amongst the British officers and governors of the country. It can be analysed under three headings: political, social and religious, and military. The first two headings apply to general unrest which afforded a favourable climate for the third.

The political causes were undoubtedly the annexations by Lord Dalhousie (Governor-General 1848–56) and his revival of the 'doctrine of lapse', whereby dependant states reverted to British rule in the event of there being no natural heir of the ruling family. Although necessary as reforms, in view of the large vested interest of the Honourable East India Company, these annexations alienated the greater majority of the local rulers and instilled fear and uncertainty, as in the case of Oudh and the absorption of the great states of the Maratha pentarchy which left hardly anything of the old Mughal Empire. In effect the annexations narrowed the field in which native Indians could have any political or administrative influence.

The devout Hindu, more especially his priests, considered that the power of the British was

Enfield rifle was introduced into India to replace the unrifled India pattern Brown Bess musket. Although still a muzzle-loader, the Enfield could be loaded more quickly and was far more accurate at a much longer range. With this new rifle came a novel cartridge made up with the ball and gunpowder in a narrow paper cylinder, which was heavily greased to keep the paper dry and for ease of loading. To charge the Enfield rifle, the weapon was held in the left hand. The top of the cartridge was bitten or torn off and the powder poured into the rifle. Then the bullet, still inside the cardboard cylinder, was rammed down the barrel, its passage being facilitated by the coating of grease round the base. Early in January 1857, a low-caste Lascar working at the arsenal at Dum-Dum asked a Brahmin sepoy of the garrison to give him a drink from his *lotah* (a brass drinking bowl). The Brahmin refused, saying that the bowl would be contaminated by the lips of one of a lower caste. Nettled by the reply, the Lascar retorted that the sepoy would soon lose his caste altogether as the Government were manufacturing cartridges for the new rifle smeared with the fat of cows and pigs. The rumour quickly spread and with it horror, for the cow is sacred to the Hindu and the pig unclean to the Mohammedan. To the sepoys it appeared that the British were really bent on breaking their adherence to religious traditions.

During the first four months of 1857, the initial rumblings of the storm were heard: outbreaks of incendiarism occurred at Barrackpore and the 19th Bengal Native Infantry was disbanded. On 29 March a more serious incident occurred at Barrackpore. Mangal Pande, a sepoy of the 34th Native Infantry, was causing a furore, probably under the influence of some drug, and calling on his comrades to join him and die for their religion and caste. While resisting arrest he wounded the regimental Sergeant-Major and the Adjutant before he was finally disarmed by Major-General Hearsey. Mangal Pande was tried by court-martial and hanged, and the 34th partially disbanded.

By the beginning of May 1857 the Army of the Bengal Presidency teetered on the brink of mutiny. A letter, written by Captain Martineau of the Musketry Depot at Ambala, uncannily

3. **An Enfield rifle cartridge, c. 1857.**

defined the causes and implications of the impending catastrophe: 'Feeling . . . is as bad as can be and matters have gone so far that I can hardly devise any suitable remedy. We make a grand mistake in supposing that because we dress, arm and drill Hindustani soldiers as Europeans, they become one bit European in their feelings and ideas. I see them on parade for say two hours daily, but what do I know of them for the other 22? What do they talk about in their lines, what do they plot? For all I can tell I might as well be in Siberia. I know that at the present moment an unusual agitation is pervading the ranks of the entire native army, but what it will exactly result in, I am afraid to say. I can detect the near approach of the storm, I can hear the moaning of the hurricane, but I can't say how, when, or where it will break forth.

'Why, whence the danger, you say. Everywhere far and near, the army under some maddening impulse, are looking out with strained expectation for something, some unseen invisible agency has caused one common electric thrill to run thro' all. I don't think they know themselves what they will do, or that they have any plan of action except of resistance to invasion of their religion and their faith. But, good God! Here are all the elements of combustion at hand, 100,000 men, sullen distrustful, fierce, with all their deepest and inmost sympathies, as well as worst passions, roused, and we thinking to cajole them into good humour by patting them on the back, saying what a fool you are for making such a fuss about nothing. They no longer believe us, they have passed out of restraint and will be off at a gallop before long.

'If a flare-up from any cause takes place at one station, it will spread and become universal.'

5

4. Duffadar of the 9th Bengal Irregular Cavalry, c.1852.

Meerut

The flare-up occurred at Meerut, one of the largest and most important military stations in India, some thirty miles from Delhi. Meerut seemed the most unlikely place for an insurrection as it was one of the few stations where British troops were almost as numerous as those of the Company's Bengal Army. There were some 2,200 British troops made up of the 6th Dragoon Guards, the 1st Battalion 60th Rifles, a troop of Horse Artillery, a battery of Field Artillery and a company of Foot Artillery. The three Indian regiments, amounting to less than 3,000 men, were the 11th and 20th Native Infantry and the 3rd Light Cavalry.

On 24 April Colonel Carmichael Smyth, the zealous but unpopular commander of the 3rd Light Cavalry, held a parade of the ninety skirmishers in order to explain to them that they need no longer bite the cartridge but could tear or pinch it with their fingers. Only five out of the ninety men accepted the cartridge offered. The circumstances were reported to the officer commanding the station and the General commanding the division, who ordered that the eighty-five skirmishers should be tried by court-martial. Fifteen native officers, six Mohammedans and nine Hindus, were appointed and, with only one dissenter, found the sowars guilty and sentenced them to ten years' hard labour.

A general punishment parade was ordered at daybreak on the 9 May, at which all the troops in the cantonment were present, and drawn up to form three sides of a hollow square. Facing each other were the 60th Rifles in their dark green uniforms and the 6th Dragoon Guards in their plumed brass helmets and blue tunics. The third side was formed by the 11th and 20th Bengal Native Infantry and, dismounted, the 3rd Light Cavalry. Positioned behind the square was a light field battery and a troop of Bengal Horse Artillery. Although the Indian troops were armed their ammunition pouches, by order, were empty.

With the arrival of Major-General Hewitt the eighty-five prisoners were marched onto the parade ground by their escort, where they were stripped of their uniforms, placed in irons by the armourers and smiths of the artillery and then marched off to jail, shouting reproaches to their comrades and curses at their commanding officers.

During the evening of 9 May, Lieutenant Hugh Gough, son of the Commander-in-Chief in the Sikh Wars, who had recently joined the 3rd Light Cavalry, was paid a visit by a native officer of his troop who warned him that the next day the men would mutiny, break into the jail and release their comrades. Gough immediately reported to his commanding officer, Colonel Carmichael Smyth, who 'treated the communication with contempt, reproving me for listening to such idle words'. Gough was convinced that the native officer was telling the truth so he tried again, this time repeating his story to Brigadier Archdale Wilson, the artillery officer who commanded the station, but there the reception was no better.

The morning and afternoon of the next day, Sunday 10 May, passed without incident. It was not until between five and six o'clock, as the British were preparing either for the evening service at St John's Church or to listen to the band in the park, that the Meerut cantonments were plunged into an orgy of blood and fire that marked the true beginning of the Mutiny.

In the dark, narrow streets of the bazaar the sowars of the 3rd Light Cavalry, indignant but still calm, were discussing the humiliation of their comrades and considering ways of obtaining a re-trial. Goaded by the jeers of civilians and prostitutes, who reproached them for failing to help their brothers-in-arms, their tempers rose until it only needed the slightest provocation to light the flame of revolt. It was not long in coming. On their drill ground the 60th Rifles, dressed in whites and wearing only side-arms,

5. Conductor Buckley, who took part in the defence of the Delhi Magazine and helped Lieutenants Forrest and Willoughby to blow it up when all hope was gone.

were preparing for church parade. A native cook boy misconstrued the parade's intentions and quickly spread the story that the British were assembling to attack and put in irons all the sepoys and sowars they could find. Immediately the cavalrymen armed and mounted and made for the jail. As they charged up to the jail the native guards fled, leaving the way clear for the deliverance of the eighty-five skirmishers. Unfortunately, hundreds of civil prisoners were also set free and mingled with the sowars, and in a few minutes turned the freedom-fighters into a

6. Atkinson lithograph of British troops on the march towards Delhi. Note typical 'shirtsleeve order', rolled trousers, curtained forage caps, etc.

wild mob with a thirst for revenge, murder and destruction.

The murder that set the seal on the rebellion was that of Colonel John Finnis, the commanding officer of the 11th Native Infantry. He had ridden down to the infantry lines to try and calm his men, who were still uncertain as to where their loyalties lay. As he was talking to them a sepoy of the 20th Native Infantry raised his musket and fired. Almost immediately other sepoys followed suit and Finnis toppled from his horse, riddled with bullets. Seeing the fate of their commander the 11th threw in their lot with the mutineers and began to set fire to their lines.

As the infantry lines and European bungalows were set to the torch men, women and children were murdered in the most horrible circumstances. Prompt action on the part of the British might have averted the many atrocities committed that evening, but from the outset the military commanders were caught off balance. The

60th Rifles, instead of being brought into action at once, were sent to change into their green uniforms, as the sergeant-major deemed white drills unsuitable for street fighting. Once they had changed there was a further delay as the roll was called. The Carabiniers were, by error, sent to the jail and not to the native parade grounds.

As night fell the mutineers began to make their way towards Delhi, but there was no attempt at pursuit by the British. 'Our military authorities were paralysed . . .' wrote an eye-witness, 'No one knew what was best to do, and nothing was done. The rebels had it all their own way . . .' As Meerut blazed, the senile and obese General Hewitt and his second in command, Archdale Wilson, marshalled the entire European garrison on the 60th Rifles' parade ground and kept them there to 'repel an attack', remaining deaf to the pleas of Custance and Rosser of the Carabiniers, Jones of the 60th and Tombs of the Artillery, that they be allowed to follow the mutineers. Many of the other officers were also galled by the lack of action; Hugh Gough was convinced that if a pursuit had been carried out Delhi would have

been saved. In his official despatch, General Hewitt gave few details of the uprising and no information as to why there was no advance made in pursuit of the rebels. All through the night the dissidents pressed on towards Delhi, the former capital of the Mughal Empire, and early on the morning of 11 May the first of them, sowars of the 3rd Light Cavalry, thundered across the Bridge of Boats that spanned the River Jumna and up to the city walls.

Delhi

There were no European regiments at Delhi, and the majority of the sepoys there were only too ready to join the revolt. Lieutenant Edward Vibart of the 54th Native Infantry was an eye-witness to the day's events.

'The orderly havildar of my company came running up to my bungalow to report that the regiment had received orders to march down

7. Raiding party of Fusiliers bringing captured rebel guns into the camp on Delhi Ridge. Note interesting details, such as pepperbox pistol in belt of officer waving helmet and sword from first limber.

instantly to the city, as some troopers of the 3rd Light Cavalry had that morning arrived from Meerut and were creating disturbances. Hurrying on my uniform, and ordering my pony to be saddled, I without loss of time galloped down to the parade-ground, and saw the regiment falling in by companies and preparing to start. Colonel Ripley, our Commandant, who appeared much excited, was already there and giving directions. The Grenadiers and No. 1 (the latter my company) were ordered to proceed under command of Major Patterson to the artillery lines, in order to escort a couple of guns to the city. We accordingly marched off at once; the rest of the regiment, with the band playing, followed shortly afterwards. Arriving at the artillery lines, Major Paterson was informed by Captain de Tessier that the guns were not quite ready, but that if we proceeded quietly towards the city, they would overtake us at the gallop. Major Paterson,

9

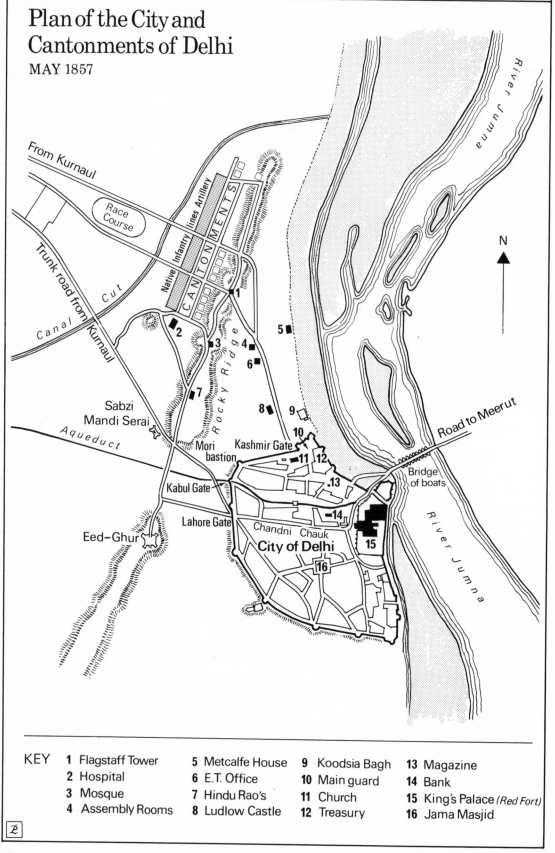

Plan of the City and Cantonments of Delhi
MAY 1857

From Kurnaul

Trunk road from Kurnaul

Canal Cut

Race Course

Native Infantry Lines Artillery

CANTONMENTS

N

1

2

3 4

5

6

7

8 9

10

Sabzi Mandi Serai

Aqueduct

Rocky Ridge

Mori bastion

Kashmir Gate

11 12

.13

Kabul Gate

Eed-Ghur

Lahore Gate

Chandni Chauk

City of Delhi

14

15

16

River Jumna

Road to Meerut

Bridge of boats

River Jumna

KEY

1	Flagstaff Tower	**5**	Metcalfe House	**9**	Koodsia Bagh	**13** Magazine
2	Hospital	**6**	E.T. Office	**10**	Main guard	**14** Bank
3	Mosque	**7**	Hindu Rao's	**11**	Church	**15** King's Palace *(Red Fort)*
4	Assembly Rooms	**8**	Ludlow Castle	**12**	Treasury	**16** Jama Masjid

8. Sketch of a loyal Punjab trooper of Hodson's Horse in 1857.

however, determined to wait. The regiment, meanwhile, with Colonel Ripley at their head, left us behind, and proceeded towards the Kashmir Gate and Main Guard.

'After a delay of about twenty minutes we were joined by the two guns, under the command of Lieutenant Wilson, and our two companies, with the guns, then proceeded on as fast as possible to the city. We were still some distance off when the sound of musketry was distinctly heard, and now, as the church tower came in view, we could plainly see smoke arising around it, and that our regiment was actively engaged in that locality.

'Pushing on at all speed, we shortly afterwards met Captain Wallace, of the 54th Native Infantry, the field officer of the week, coming out of the Kashmir Gate and riding back towards cantonments. He implored us for "God's sake" to hurry on as fast as possible, as all the 54th officers were being shot down by cavalry troopers, and their men were making no effort to defend them. On hearing this startling news, Major Paterson desired

9. **Lieutenant Clifford Meecham and Assistant Surgeon Thomas Anderson with a party of loyal Sikh cavalrymen; note characteristic details of costume. Meecham served with Hodson's Horse throughout the defence of the Lucknow Residency.**

me to halt and load. The guns were then advanced through the gate, followed by the infantry.

'At that moment the body of our unfortunate Colonel was carried out, literally hacked to pieces. One arm just below the shoulder was almost severed. Such a fearful sight I never beheld. The poor man was still alive, and, though scarcely able to articulate, I distinctly gathered from the few words he gasped out, that we had no chance against the cavalry troopers, and that our own men had turned against us . . .

'A consultation was now held to decide what was best to be done. At length it was determined to hold the Main Guard . . .

'At length some of us advanced beyond the inner gates, and the first thing I saw was the lifeless body of Captain Burrowes lying close by the gate of the churchyard. Assisted by a couple of

sepoys, I carried him into the main garden and laid him on a *charpoy*. Other bodies were now observed scattered about the place. Five were at length found and brought in. Also a sepoy shot through the arm. These were poor Burrowes, Smith, Edwards, and Waterfield, all of my own regiment. The fifth was one of the European sergeants attached to the corps; he was the only one alive. A ball had shattered his leg, and he had another frightful wound on his head. Since then I have witnessed many painful sights, but I shall never forget my feelings that day as I saw our poor fellows being brought in, their faces distorted with all the agonies of a violent death, and hacked about in every conceivable way . . .

'Reports now reached us that, besides the 3rd Light Cavalry troopers, two regiments of native infantry, the 11th and 20th, had also arrived from Meerut, and were on their way to attack us . . .

'In this state of disquieting suspense, the first hour passed by, and we were speculating on the possible fate of the rest of the officers of the 54th, when, to my great joy, Lieutenant Osborn, our Adjutant, and Captain Butler suddenly made their appearance. The latter was besmearched with blood, and was faint from a blow he had received on the head from a large brickbat. We now learnt some particulars of the events of the morning.

'It appeared that no sooner had the regiment advanced through the Kashmir Gate into the open space in front of the church, than they were assailed by about twenty troopers dressed in uniform. These men shouted out to the sepoys that they had no intention of hurting them, but had merely come to slaughter the accursed *Feringhees*. Our officers were then sabred and shot down. Vainly they called on their men to fire on the troopers: these miscreants, on the contrary, immediately joined with the insurgents, and some of the cowardly traitors actually bayonetted Colonel Ripley after he was unhorsed and cut down. In the midst of this confusion, Osborn and Butler escaped down one of the streets, but here they were attacked by the populace, who came out with stones and bricks to assail them. Never-theless, after passing through several streets, these two officers managed to escape outside the city walls, and hence made their way to us in safety . . .

'Intimation was received about this time that Mr Fraser, the Commissioner, who on hearing of the arrival of the mutineers in the morning had at once gone down to the palace, and Captain Douglas, the Commandant of the Palace Guards, had both been murdered. Mr Jennings, the chaplain, and his daughter, Miss Jennings, together with a friend, Miss Clifford, who was residing with them inside the palace walls, we heard had also shared the same fate. It was evident that every European who came across the mutineers was immediately shot down and killed.'

As Delhi was given over to the same orgy of bloodshed and looting that had been witnessed at Meerut, those who could, made their way up the dusty road to the Ridge, a rocky spine of land two miles to the north-west of the city, where, on the instructions of Brigadier Harry Graves the senior British officer, they were assembled at the

10. **The advance of the long-awaited siege train towards Delhi, guarded by loyal Punjabi troops.**

11. Surprise attacks by the sepoys on the British line along Delhi Ridge obliged the besiegers to maintain constant watch. Here, an outlying picket – probably of Fusiliers, judging from the grenade motif on the belt-plates – is made up of men taking their turn on guard and others sleeping.

Flagstaff Tower, a 150-foot spire overlooking the city. Those civilians who had hesitated to move became the victims of the bloodthirsty mob that surged through the streets.

By the late afternoon the British on the Ridge began to eye the Indian troops with them with anxiety and had great doubts about whether to trust them or not, for they were all aware that the main magazine, three miles outside the city, had been taken over by the mutineers. It had been guarded by native troops who had not hesitated to throw in their lot with the rebels. At about 4 pm a terrific explosion rent the air and a dense column of smoke billowed up as a smaller magazine, some six hundred yards from the Kashmir Gate, was blown sky-high by a group of British officers under Lieutenant Willoughby. Having resisted the mutineers against impossible odds until deserted by their native troops, and on the point of being

overrun as the sepoys swarmed over the walls from ladders supplied by the Palace, the tiny force of Europeans calmly chose death rather than allow the magazine to fall into enemy hands. Amazingly, a handful of scorched and dazed survivors escaped to the British lines.

As the magazine exploded the sepoys who had remained faithfully with the British on the Ridge, grabbed their weapons and rushed to the city, passing as they went the last of the refugees from the city. Without them, all was lost, the Ridge would have to be evacuated. As night fell the British force began to move off. On horseback and foot, in bullock carts and carriages they made their way from the Ridge to seek safety at Karnaul, Ambala and Meerut. In the space of eight hours, the mutineers had captured a city of immense symbolic importance.

The news of the outbreak at Delhi reached Ambala over the telegraph during the afternoon of 11 May, but it was not until the following day that the telegram reached the Commander-in-Chief, General Anson, at Simla. Immediately he despatched orders for troops to move in the direction

of Delhi. Brigadier Archdale Wilson was to march from Meerut and join up with a column from Ambala.

12. Mutineers in an entrenchment. Most sepoys seem to have reverted to white native clothing. The beads worn at the throat are a frequently mentioned feature.

When Anson arrived at Ambala on 15 May, he found telegrams from Canning and other notables urging him, rather obviously, to retake Delhi as soon as possible. Unfortunately there was still a lot of work to be done before an advance could be made for there was a deplorable lack of transport and supplies. The first section of troops began to move off on 17 May and by the 30th all the force had arrived at Karnaul. However, they arrived with a new commander, for Anson had succumbed to cholera on the 27th, after handing over his command to Sir Henry Barnard, a man of advanced years but who had at least seen some action in the Crimea, as Lord Raglan's Chief of Staff. Without delay the column moved on to meet Wilson and the force from Meerut, which it did at Baghpat. On 8 June a sharp engagement took place at Badli-ke-serai, some six miles from Delhi, where a force of about 30,000 mutineers were entrenched. After the rebels had been driven from their position the column pressed on and occupied the old military cantonments on the Ridge. Foolishly, Barnard ordered the burning of the old native troop lines as a gesture of defiance and retribution, an act that was later regretted, as the buildings would have offered much-needed protection against the fierce sun in the months to come.

The British troops now began to settle in along the Ridge, occupying a number of strong-points: the Flagstaff Tower, a mosque, the observatory and near the extreme right of their position, a large mansion, Hindu Rao's house. Between these buildings and the city walls was a space overgrown with trees and shrubs and dotted with old mosques, tombs and ruins, which afforded ample cover for the mutineers. In this area were two buildings held by the rebels, the Metcalf House and Ludlow Castle, the former being the old residence of Sir Theo Metcalf, the joint magistrate, and the latter the home of Simon Fraser, the Commissioner of Delhi, who had been murdered

13. The storming of the Kashmir Gate, Delhi, on 14 September 1857 by a mixed force under Colonel George Campbell.

when the Meerut insurgents entered the city.

From their encampment on the Ridge the British looked down onto the city which, with its seven miles of twenty-four-foot high walls strengthened by a number of bastions and ten massive gates, seemed a near insurmountable problem. Around the wall ran a dry ditch, twenty-five feet deep and almost as broad. Not only were the gates well protected but the bastions were mounted with 114 guns, mostly twenty-four pounders, against which the British had 2,900 troops and twenty-eight field guns. With the meagre force at his disposal all Barnard could do was watch the portion that faced the Ridge, barely a seventh of the whole, leaving the river front open to receive supplies and rebel reinforcements throughout the siege. 'We came to besiege Delhi . . .' noted one observer, 'but . . . in reality we were the besieged . . . the mutineers the besiegers.'

The problem facing Barnard was whether, with inferior numbers, he could attempt to carry out the expectations of the Government and

his fellow countrymen by capturing Delhi without delay. Against his better judgement, for he knew that his career was the price of failure, Barnard agreed to make an attack on the 12–13 June. Unfortunately the element of surprise was lost when Brigadier Graves, the field officer of the day, refused to accept a verbal message and galloped to Barnard's tent for further instructions. During the discussion that followed, Graves explained that in his view it might be possible to take the city but with such a small force it would be impossible to hold it. As dawn broke Barnard abandoned the plan for the assault.

So the British continued to wait on the Ridge. 'The heat was insupportable . . .' remembered Lieutenant C. J. Griffiths, 'the thermometer under the shade of my tent marking 112 degrees; and to add to our misery there came upon us a plague of flies, the like of which I verily believe had not been on the earth since Moses in that manner brought down the wrath of God on the Egyptians. They literally darkened the sky, descending in myriads and covering everything in our midst. Foul and loathsome they were, and we knew that they owed their existence to, and fattened on, the putrid corpses of dead men and animals which lay rotting and unburied in every direction. The air was tainted with corruption, and the heat was intense. Can it, then, be wondered that pestilence increased daily in the camp, claiming its victims from every regiment, native as well as European?'

One of these European victims was General Barnard who was struck down by cholera on 5 July, and died within a few hours. His successor was General T. Reed who held the command for a fortnight before being despatched to the hills on sick leave, handing over to Brigadier Archdale Wilson, who had shown his complete lack of initiative at Meerut.

All this time the rebels had been making frequent sorties, some directed at the Ludlow Castle and the Metcalf house which the British had occupied to protect their flank, but the greatest number of attacks were directed at Hindu Rao's house which was gallantly defended, and held throughout the siege, by a group of Gurkhas.

The most powerful of the rebel assaults took place on 23 June, the anniversary of Clive's victory at the battle of Plassey, for it was this day that the fakirs predicted would see the end of British rule in India. 'We were ordered under arms at 3 a.m. . . .' wrote Lieutenant Henry Parlett Bishop of the Bengal Horse Artillery, 'and remained so until 6 a.m. when I went with my division to relieve the picket at the Flagstaff; a large column of the enemy to the number of 7,000 had come out from the fort, and apparently wished to work round to our rear by our right flank, in this they were thwarted by the bridges on the trunk road having been blown up. They then took up a position with their guns to enfilade our battery at Hindoo Rao's house. A party composed of the 60th Rifles, 1st and 2nd Europeans, Guides and Goorkhas were sent to carry the position, in this they failed, and hard fighting went on all day in the gardens and masonry serais of the suburbs with various success, in which we lost many men . . .'

14. The Kashmir Gate, Delhi.

Reinforcements were slowly arriving in the British camp and by the beginning of July the force had increased to about 6,600 men. Unfortunately losses were very heavy indeed; in one week alone, during the month of July, twenty-five officers and four hundred men were either wounded or killed. So the months passed. The rainy season began and transformed the camp into a quagmire, but still the British hung on grimly and waited impatiently for the reinforcements that would at last enable them to launch a successful assault on the city.

In the early weeks of August Brigadier John Nicholson, with a mobile column of 4,200 men, arrived from Lahore and received a tremendous welcome from the troops on the Ridge. On 24 August Nicholson had his first brush with the Dehli mutineers. Knowing that a siege-train was on the way a large force, with eighteen guns, was despatched from Delhi to intercept it. The next morning Nicholson, with a selected force, rode

out in pursuit and despite heavy rainfall caught up with them at Najafgarh. Lieutenant Griffiths was with the pursuing force. 'When we halted, Nicholson came to the front and, addressing the regiments of European infantry, spoke a few soul-words, calling on us to reserve our fire till close to the enemy's batteries, and then to charge with fixed bayonets. He was answered with a cheer, and the lines advanced across the plain, steady and unbroken, as though on parade.

'The enemy had opened fire, and were answered by our guns, the infantry marched with sloped arms at the quickstep till within one hundred yards, when we delivered a volley. Then the war-cry of the British soldiers was heard, and the two regiments came to the charge, and ran at the double towards the serai.

'Lieutenant Gabbett, of my regiment, was the first man to reach the entrenchment, and, passing through the embrasure, received a bayonet thrust in the left breast, which stretched him on

15. Mounted British and Indian officers supervise the attack on the Kashmir Gate.

the ground. The men followed, clearing everything before them, capturing the four guns in the serai, bayoneting the rebels and firing on those who had taken to flight at our approach. Then, changing front, the whole force swept along the entrenchment to the bridge, making a clean sweep of the enemy, who turned and fled, leaving the remaining nine guns in our hands.

'Our Horse Artillery, under Major Tombs, mowed down the fugitives in hundreds, and continued following and firing on them till darkness set in. The cavalry also – a squadron of the gallant 9th Lancers, with the Guides and Punjabees – did their share of work, while the European infantry were nobly supported by the corps of Punjab Rifles, who cleared the town of sepoys.

'The battle had lasted a very short time, and after dark we bivouacked in the pouring rain, completely exhausted from our long march and subsequent fighting, and faint from want of food, none of which passed our lips for more than sixteen hours.

'Still, the day's work was not done. A village to the rear was found to be occupied by the enemy. The Punjab Rifles were ordered to take it. They

16. Atkinson lithograph of street fighting during the storming of Delhi. Note British and Sikh infantry; and officer spiking cannon on the left.

met with a most obstinate resistance, their young commander, Lumsden, being killed. The General then sent part of my regiment to dislodge the rebels, but we met with only partial success, and had one officer, named Elkington, mortally wounded, the enemy evacuating the place during the night.'

British losses during the battle of Najafgarh were two officers and twenty-three men killed and two officers and sixty-eight men wounded. The next morning Nicholson formed up the column and marched back to the Ridge at Delhi, where there was great rejoicing at the first victory since Badli-ke-serai some two months before.

On 4 September the long awaited siege-train arrived. H. P. Bishop wrote that it consisted of '. . . 22 pieces, 4, 10 inch mortars, 4, 8 inch howitzers, 6, 24 pounders and 8, 18 pounders escorted by about 200 of the 8th Foot and a wing of the Belooch Battalion.' With the British force almost doubled, General Wilson was put under

17. Lieutenant-Colonel Edward Greathead commanded the 8th Foot (The King's Regiment) in the siege of Delhi, and later led a mobile column.

that it could be ascended with ease.

'Fifty guns and mortars were now pouring shot and shell without a moment's interval on the doomed city. The din and roar were deafening; day and night salvoes of artillery were heard, roll following roll in endless succession, and striking terror in the hearts of those who felt that the day of retribution was at hand.'

A reconnaissance report, made on the night of 13 September, stated that two breaches, one on the right of the Kashmir Gate and the other to the left of the Water Bastion, were practicable and orders for an assault were immediately issued. Generally speaking the plan of attack was firstly, with the aid of scaling ladders, to cross the ditch that surrounded the city and then to take up defensible positions at the wall itself. This achieved, the succeeding operations were to be determined by the commanders themselves, it being understood that the goal was to enter the

18. Macabre accessory for a portrait photograph of Thomas Ray wearing a typical British officer's uniform of the Mutiny; note Indian sword, and revolver with lanyard.

tremendous pressure from Nicholson and others to launch an all-out assault. Finally, Wilson reluctantly agreed.

Within four days and nights the guns and mortars were in position, and on 11 September all was ready. 'At length the whole of our batteries opened fire on the city bastions and walls. The Kashmir Bastion was soon silenced, the ramparts and adjacent curtains knocked to fragments, and a large breach opened in the walls. On the extreme left, at the Custom House, our battery was only 180 yards from the city, and the crushing fire from this, when in full play, smashed to pieces the Water Bastion, overturned the guns, and made a breach in the curtain so wide and practicable

19. Cadets in front of the East India Company's College at Addiscombe.

narrow streets of the city and make for the King's palace. There were to be five storming columns:

No. 1: One thousand men under the command of Brigadier-General John Nicholson were to storm the breach near the Kashmir Gate and escalade the bastion.

No. 2: Eight hundred and fifty men under Brigadier William Jones of the 61st Regiment were assigned the breach near the Water Bastion.

No. 3: Nine hundred and fifty men commanded by Colonel George Campbell were to assault the Kashmir Gate after a party of Engineers led by Lieutenants Home and Salkeld had blown it in.

No. 4: Eight hundred and sixty men under Major Charles Reid, supported by twelve hundred Sikhs of the Maharajah of Kashmir, were to fight their way through the eastern suburbs and enter the city by the Kabul Gate which was to be opened from the inside by Nicholson's men.

No. 5: Commanded by Brigadier Longfield, some thirteen hundred men were to cover the advance of Nicholson's column and form a reserve.

As the troops began to fall in for the attack the batteries reopened their fire, for it was necessary to clear the breaches which the mutineers had partially filled in during the night. At length the signal was given and while the heavy guns still thundered at the breaches, answered by the guns from the city, the columns moved silently and steadily down. After consulting with Brigadier Jones, Nicholson gave the signal to attack. Some five thousand British and Indian troops, under a hail of grape-shot and musket balls, fought their way through the breaches and into the city, which by nightfall was partially occupied. The losses were heavy: 66 officers and 1,104 men were killed and wounded, including Nicholson. He had been mortally wounded in a narrow alley by the Kashmir Gate, and lingered on in agony for another nine days while heavy street fighting continued in the city. He died on 23 September, after a salute from the King's palace announced that Delhi was in British hands once more.

21

Cawnpore

About 260 miles to the east of Delhi and situated on the south bank of the River Ganges was the important trading centre and military station of Cawnpore. Like most stations at that time Cawnpore was divided into three distinct areas: the native city with its narrow streets and bazaars; the civil lines consisting of the administrative offices, jail, treasury, church and the bungalows of the European inhabitants; and the military lines, which in this case were situated to the west of the native city and separated from it by a canal. In 1857 Cawnpore was the headquarters of the military command for the province of Oudh and the area known as the Doab. However there were very few European troops stationed there; only about three hundred, in contrast with some three thousand native troops belonging to the 1st, 53rd, and 56th Bengal Native Infantry regiments and the 2nd Cavalry. The station was commanded by General Sir Hugh Wheeler, an old man with fifty-four years service in India behind him, who was considered to be one of the most experienced and best Generals in the East India Company's army.

About six miles to the north-west of Cawnpore, in the town of Bithur, lived Nana Sahib, the eldest adopted son of Baji Rao who was the last titular leader of the Maharatha confederacy. Nana Sahib was trusted by Wheeler who had himself taken an Indian wife. But Nana had a grievance against the British. Forty years before, his father had challenged British power and failed, and in 1818 surrendered on terms which included his exile to Bithur and a yearly pension of 800,000 rupees. When he died in 1851 he left his title and estates to Nana but the Government abolished the title and with it, the annual pension. Repeated appeals to ascending levels of authority failed to secure a reversal of this decision. This treatment rankled in Nana Sahib's mind and gave him a thirst for vengeance against those who refused to acknowledge his supposed rights.

When the first news of the mutiny at Meerut and the possession of Delhi by the rebels reached

20. **Sir James Outram (1803–1863), the 'Bayard of India', commanded the Dinapore and Cawnpore Divisions of the Bengal Army during the Mutiny, and was Chief Commander for Oudh, August 1857–April 1858.**

Cawnpore it seemed to have no immediate effect on the sepoys. Nevertheless, Wheeler made preparations to protect the European and Eurasian population against any impending rising. The garrison at that time was almost without any but native troops, the only British regiment having been sent, a short time before, to Lucknow where the 7th Oudh Irregulars had caused some trouble.

There were two possible defensible locations. The magazine, a few miles to the north of the city, contained large stocks and ammunition but, in Wheeler's view, was too far from the river up which, he was sure, reinforcements would arrive. the second location, and the one chosen by Wheeler, was a pair of barrack blocks, one of masonry and the other with a thatched roof, which stood out in the open away from the native city and close to the road from Allahabad. The reasons for his choice were that the magazine would be hard for a relieving column to reach and he had been assured, whether by Nana Sahib or his spies is not sure, that if the troops did revolt they would march to Delhi and not bother to attack the Europeans at Cawnpore. Wheeler immediately ordered the erection of a parapet and gun emplacements around the buildings. With the Indians sullen and rebellious it was difficult to find the necessary workmen for the job, which resulted in a loosely-built earthwork about four feet high that was not even bullet-proof at the crest. There was also a shortage of water, for although there was a plentiful supply nearby, insufficient had been moved into the defence area.

Towards the end of May Wheeler, expecting trouble at any moment, ordered the civilians into the entrenchment and appealed to Henry Lawrence at Lucknow for reinforcements. Lawrence despatched eighty-four men of the 32nd Foot (Queen's) and two squadrons of irregulars under the command of Captain Fletcher Hayes. Writing in a letter to Lucknow, Hayes painted a very gloomy picture of the situation when he arrived. 'At six a.m. I went out to have a look at the various places, and since I have been in India never witnessed so frightful a scene of confusion, fright,

and bad arrangement as the European barracks presented. Four guns were in position loaded, with European artillery-men in nightcaps and wide-awakes and side-arms . . . looking like melodramatic buccaneers. People of all kinds, of every colour, sect and profession, were crowding into the barracks . . . I saw quite enough to convince me that if any insurrection took or takes place, we shall have no-one to thank but ourselves, because we have now shown the natives how very easily we can become frightened, and when frightened utterly helpless.' A few days later Captain Hayes was killed when his irregulars mutinied.

The tiny force at Wheeler's disposal consisted of sixty European artillerymen with six guns, seventy invalids and eighty-four men of the 32nd Foot, about two hundred unattached officers and civilians and forty musicians belonging to the native regiments. There were also about 330 women and children. Against the repeated advice of Henry Lawrence, Wheeler continued to have complete trust in his friend Nana Sahib and he appealed to him for aid. Nana sent about

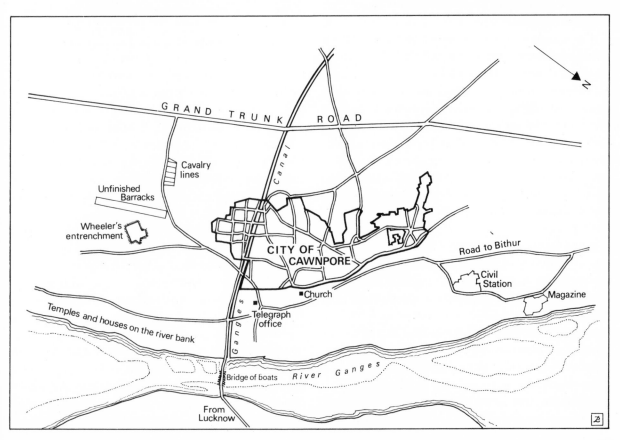

21. **Part of General Wheeler's shell-pocked position at Cawnpore – the outer face of one of the two large barrack blocks which formed the centrepiece of his entrenchment.**

three hundred men of his personal bodyguard with two guns, who were entrusted with the defence of the Treasury and the magazine. Wheeler was so convinced of their trustworthiness that when the first of the reinforcements arrived, one hundred men of the 84th Foot (Queen's), he sent half of them on to Henry Lawrence at Lucknow, believing their assurances that other troops were on the way.

The situation remained calm, but not for long. On the night of 4 June, the 2nd Cavalry and the 1st Bengal Native Infantry mutinied and joined Nana Sahib's men in looting the Treasury. The other two native infantry regiments remained loyal throughout the night but mutinied early the next morning. The 53rd were preparing their breakfast when Wheeler, convinced that they were about to attack, ordered his artillery to open fire on their lines, which in seconds converted the majority of a potentially loyal regiment to the rebel cause.

After setting fire to the Government offices, releasing prisoners from the jail and plundering the treasury, the insurgents marched off on the road to Delhi. The sepoys got no further than Kullianpur before being persuaded to return to Cawnpore to attack the entrenchment. Whether the Nana's *volte face* was intended from the beginning or whether he was menaced by the mutinous sepoys has never been proved. Whichever it was, Nana Sahib rode at the head of the mutineers on the road back to Cawnpore. On the morning of

6 June Nana Sahib informed General Wheeler that he was about to launch an attack on the entrenchment. Within a few hours the sepoys surrounded Wheeler's position and began an artillery bombardment, for although Wheeler had ordered the destruction of the magazine and its contents, the sepoys had prevented it. As the first round-shot crashed into the entrenchment the British Artillery under Lieutenant Ashe riposted. The siege had begun.

From 6 to 25 June, the entrenchment was under continual bombardment by day and sometimes by night. Nineteen days does not seem an unduly long time, but under an implacable, broiling sun, in overcrowded conditions and with starvation staring them in the face, the sufferings and hardships of the defenders can only be realized by reading the accounts left by the few survivors of the garrison, which paint a vivid and sometimes horrifying picture of life in the entrenchment. For Amelia Horne, then a girl of eighteen, the opening day of the siege was '. . . one of the most terrible sights which our eyes now beheld; the whole surrounding country seemed covered with men at arms, on horse and on foot, and they presented a most formidable appearance. They seemed such odds to keep at bay from our Lilliputian defences.

'The site of our entrenchment was surrounded by large and substantial buildings . . . occupied by the rebels, and from roof and window, all day, a shower of bullets poured down on us in our exposed position. Shell likewise kept falling all over the entrenchment . . . One shell killed seven women as it fell hissing into the trenches and burst. Windows and doors were soon shot off their sockets, and the shot and shell began to play freely through the denuded buildings . . .'

Despite the occasional morale-raising sortie against the rebel positions, those in the entrenchment were under no misapprehension as to the eventual outcome of their struggle, unless reinforcements arrived. On 23 June, the anniversary of the battle of Plassey, the rebels made a concerted effort to take the entrenchment, but were thrown back in disorder. The next day Wheeler managed to send out a last poignant appeal for help to Henry Lawrence. 'British spirit alone remains, but it cannot last forever . . . We have no instruments, no medicines . . . casualties have been

1 **Officer, 24th Regiment of Foot
(2nd Warwickshire)**
2 **Private, 7th Regiment of Foot
(Royal Fusiliers)**
3 **Sowar, Bengal Light Cavalry**

G. A. EMBLETON

A

1 British officer, 2nd Punjab Cavalry (Probyn's Horse)
2 Private, 1st Madras Fusiliers
3 British officer
4 Private, 1st Bengal Fusiliers
5 Trooper, 9th Lancers

B

G. A. EMBLETON

1 Havildar, Nasiri Bn. (66th Goorkha Regt., Bengal Native Infantry)
2 British officer, Nasiri Bn. (66th Goorkha Regt., Bengal Native Infantry)
3 Sergeant-Major, British line infantry

G. A. EMBLETON

C

1 Sepoy, Rifle Company,
41st Bengal Native Infantry
2 Sowar, 2nd Punjab Cavalry
3 Sepoy, 41st Regiment,
Bengal Native Infantry

D

1 **Private, 91st Regiment of Foot (Argyllshire Regiment)**
2 **Officer, British line infantry**
3 **Private, 52nd Regiment of Foot (Oxfordshire Light Infantry)**

G. A. EMBLETON

E

1 Officer, Hodson's Horse
2 Captain, Naval Brigade
3 Officer, Bengal Foot Artillery

G. A. EMBLETON

1 **Private, 92nd Regiment of Foot
   (Gordon Highlanders)**
2 **Trooper, 7th Hussars**
3 **Bengal sepoy mutineer**

G. A. EMBLETON

G

H

G. A. EMBLETON

numerous . . . Surely we are not to die like rats in a cage.'

On 25 June, with the ammunition and food almost exhausted and still no sign of relief, Wheeler received a letter from Nana Sahib, brought into the entrenchment by a half-caste woman. 'All those who are in no way connected with the acts of Lord Dalhousie . . .' it read, '. . . and are willing to lay down their arms, shall receive a safe passage to Allahabad.' Wheeler was against surrender but others thought that some attempt should be made to save the women and children. After much discussion a meeting with Nana's representatives was convened for the following morning, where it was agreed that the British would surrender their guns and treasure but would be allowed to keep their hand-guns and sixty rounds of ammunition per man. In return Nana agreed to provide boats and supplies that would be waiting at the Sati Chaura Ghat on the Ganges.

At about 7 o'clock on the morning of 27 June the garrison began to move out of the entrenchment towards the river. No sooner were most of

22. The massacre at the Sati Chaura Ghat, Cawnpore. This version owes more to an understandable indignation on the part of the artist than to accuracy; it shows the firing on the refugee boats, the butchering of the women and children, and the notorious dumping of corpses in the well as being simultaneous. In fact the massacre at the Ghat took place on 27 June and the killing of the women and children on 15 July.

the civilians and wounded in the boats than the cavalry escort, provided by Nana Sahib, gave the order to open fire. The ensuing massacre was later described by Amelia Horne, one of the survivors. 'While we were endeavouring to embark the shore was lined with spectators . . . After all had embarked . . . the word was given to proceed. Instead of the crews obeying the order, a signal was given from the shore, and they all leapt into the water and waded to the bank, after having first secreted burning charcoal in the thatch of most of the boats. Immediately a volley of bullets assailed us, followed by a hail of shot and grape . . . In a few minutes pandemonium reigned. The boats were seen to be wrapped in flames, and the wounded were burnt to death. Some jumped overboard and tried to swim to the opposite shore, but were picked off by the bullets of the sepoys. Others were drowned, while a few others jumped into the water and hid behind their boats to escape the pitiless fire. But the guns continued their vile work, and grape and musketry were poured into the last mentioned people from the opposite bank which soon became alive with rebels, placed there to intercept refugees to that shore. A few succeeded in pushing their boats to the further side of the river and were mercilessly slaughtered.

'The cavalry waded into the river with drawn swords and cut down those who were still alive, while the infantry boarded the boats to loot. One unfortunate, a Mr. Kirkpatrick, in trying to ward off the blows from a sabre with his arms, had both arms chopped off. I saw him about half an hour later lying in the water still alive!

'The air resounded with the shrieks of the women and children, and agonized prayers to God for mercy. The water was red with blood, and the smoke from the heavy firing of the cannon and muskets and the fire from the burning boats lay like dense clouds all around us. Several men were mutilated in the presence of their wives, while babes and children were torn from their mother's arms and hacked to pieces . . .'

One of the boats managed to get away but only four of its passengers survived. Of the British who managed to live through the massacre on the river, the men were immediately shot but the women and children were imprisoned in a small house known as the *Bibighur*, the 'House of Ladies'. On 15 July, when news reached Cawnpore that a relieving force under General Henry Havelock was approaching the city, the rebels murdered the women and children and threw their bodies down a well. It was this final massacre that inflamed British feelings into a savage thirst for revenge; for when they entered Cawnpore, after driving out the rebels, they found the *Bibighur* looking like a slaughter-house. 'I am not exaggerating . . .' wrote one officer who had visited the place, '. . . when I tell you that the soles of my boots were more than covered with the blood of these poor wretched creatures.'

Brigadier-General Neill, almost fanatical in his desire for vengeance, issued an order that every captured rebel '. . . will be taken down to the house and will be forced to clean up a small portion of the blood-stains . . . After properly cleaning up his portion, the culprit will be immediately hanged.' Hanging, however, was thought by many to be too good for mutineers and, when facilities were available, it was usual to blow them from guns. 'It was a horrid sight . . .' wrote one eye-witness, '. . . a regular shower of human fragments of heads, of arms, of legs, appeared in the air through the smoke; and when that cleared away, these fragments lying on the ground . . . were all that remained . . .'*

Leaving Neill at Cawnpore, Havelock and his relieving force set out for the beleaguered garrison at Lucknow. Unfortunately Havelock's force, 'reduced by sickness and repeated combats . . .', was too weak to continue and was obliged to fall back on Cawnpore. It was not until the arrival of General Outram's reinforcements on 15 September, that Neill and Havelock were able to set out once more for Lucknow.

Lucknow

Sir Henry Lawrence, the Chief Commissioner of the province of Oudh, had taken up his position in Lucknow in March 1857 with the brief of trying to calm an ocean of discontent that had arisen since the Honourable East India Company had deposed the King and annexed the province in February 1856. Since the annexation the reforms that had been introduced had only increased the people's animosity towards the British. The courtiers of the old King found themselves without influence, the landowners had been deprived of large tracts of land and the villagers were more heavily taxed than ever before. These conditions had repercussions outside the province, for Oudh was the 'great nursery of sepoys'. Two-thirds of the army of the Bengal Presidency were recruited in the area, and the bad news from home was one of the major causes of their discontent in the spring of 1857.

---

*A method of execution greatly feared by the sepoys, who believed that it robbed them of an after-life.

In Lucknow, Lawrence did all in his power to set matters right but at the same time gave orders for a pentagonal entrenchment to be constructed around the Residency and for the garrison to be concentrated in that area. On 3 May, the 7th Regiment of Oudh Irregulars refused to accept the greased cartridge and Lawrence was forced to disband them. When news of the mutinies at Meerut and Delhi reached Lucknow, on 14 and 15 May Lawrence immediately asked for, and was granted, plenary power, assuming the rank of Brigadier in charge of both civil and military administration. The situation remained tense but quiet and it was not until the evening of 30 May that the expected rising occurred. Forewarned by a native that the mutiny would start at 9 p.m., the European troops managed to prevent a massacre and forced the insurgents to flee into the countryside. The next day Lawrence rode out in pursuit and managed to bring back sixty prisoners.

During the month of June, while rebellion was sweeping through the province of Oudh, the fortification of the Residency continued but, under orders from Lawrence, no attempt was made to demolish the mosques and temples near the perimeter, an error that was later to cost the lives of a number of the defenders who were sniped by rebels in these positions. When at the end of the month the garrison received the news of Wheeler's capitulation at Cawnpore, Lawrence realized that the rebel army was likely to make a move towards Lucknow. He therefore issued orders for the civilians and troops to move into the Residency entrenchment. On 29 June Lawrence was persuaded to lead an attack on an advance force of rebels near the village of Chinhat. The attack, badly planned and executed, was a near-disaster and as the British forces returned to the Residency the rebels swept forward to invest it. On 30 June one of the most famous sieges in British military history began.

Of the 3,100 people in the entrenchment the effective fighting strength was 927 Europeans and 765 Indians, but losses were heavy, for the defenders were under a concentrated rifle fire from the mosques and nearby roof-tops. On 1 July the sniper fire was supplemented by artillery and one of its first victims was Sir Henry Lawrence,

23. The Residency at Lucknow.

mortally wounded by a shell that landed in his room on the first floor of the Residency. A shell had burst in the room on the previous day, but although pressed to move to a safer place Lawrence '. . . did not believe that the enemy had an artilleryman good enough to put another shell into that small room.' He lingered on for two days and from his deathbed dictated his final orders to his successor, Colonel John Inglis, and requested that his tomb should bear the following inscription: 'Here lies Henry Lawrence who tried to do his duty. May God have mercy on him.' He was buried on the night of 4 July, in a trench along with the bodies of several other people who had been killed during the day.

Through the rains of July and August the siege continued. Attacks were repulsed, enemy mines

24. La Martinière, Lucknow, built in the Italian style in the late 18th century by a French general then employed by the ruler. At the time of the Mutiny it was used as a boys' school. It was fortified by the mutineers during Sir Colin Campbell's attack on the city.

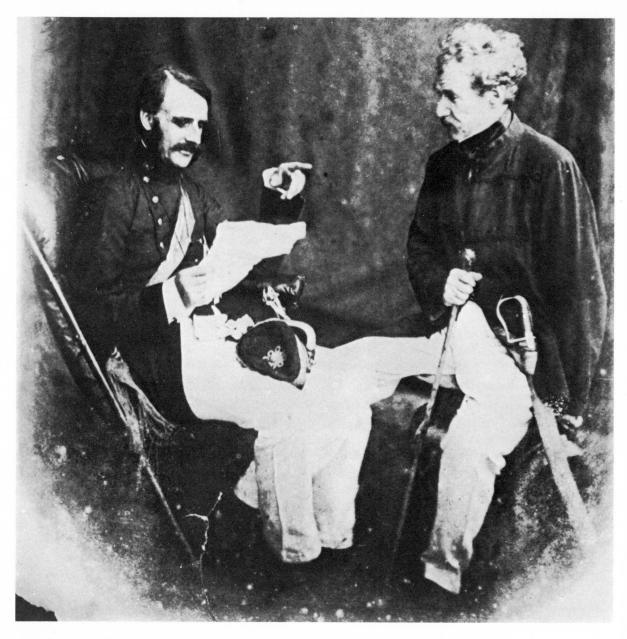

25. Major-General Mansfield, his chief of staff, 'reading a despatch' before the camera to General Sir Colin Campbell, British Commander-in-Chief in India from July 1857. A fine and greatly-loved commander, Colin Campbell fought his last campaigns during the Mutiny. His active career had begun as early as 1808, when he landed in Portugal as an ensign in the 9th Foot. He saw much action throughout the Peninsular War, in China, the Crimea, and India.

were counter-mined and nearby houses were captured and blown up. By the beginning of September matters were becoming serious, for not only was the garrison's strength declining rapidly from wounds, but smallpox and cholera had also made their appearance. However, news arrived that General Havelock was again making an advance on Lucknow after having been reinforced by troops under the command of General Sir James Outram.

Outram had in fact superseded Havelock as commander but, without the necessary authority from the government, issued an order entrusting the relief of the beleaguered garrison at Lucknow to Havelock. Outram was to accompany the force but only in his capacity as Chief Commissioner for Oudh. On 19 September the relief force crossed the Ganges and set off for Lucknow. Despite stiff opposition they fought their way into the Residency entrenchment on 27 September.

The arrival of the Outram/Havelock force was described by Mrs Harris in *A Lady's Diary of the Siege of Lucknow*. 'We had no idea they were so near, and were breathing the air in the portico as usual at that hour, at five p.m., speculating where they might be now, when suddenly, just at dusk, we heard a very sharp fire of musketry close by, and then a tremendous cheering; an instant after, the sound of bagpipes, then of soldiers running up the road. Our compound and verandah filled with our deliverers, and all of us shaking hands frantically and exchanging fervent "God bless yous!" with the gallant men and officers of the 78th Highlanders . . . the state of joyful confusion and excitement was beyond all description. The big, rough, bearded soldiers were seizing the little children out of our arms, kissing them with tears running down their cheeks, and thanking God that they had come in time to save them from the fate of those at Cawnpore . . . We were all rushing about to give the poor fellows drinks of water, for they were all perfectly exhausted . . .'

Their triumph, however, was short-lived, for nearly a third of the relieving army had been killed or wounded. Too weak to break out, Havelock and Outram found themselves in turn besieged. For another fifty-three days the mining and counter-mining, the shelling, the attacks and counter-attacks and the inevitable deaths from wounds and disease continued. Fortunately the food situation was not critical for, although on short rations, one of the relieving force discovered a *cache* of two months' supplies which Lawrence had laid down without informing his commissariat officers.

On 9 November the new Commander-in-Chief, Colin Campbell, advanced on Lucknow with an army of five thousand men. To guide this second relieving force through the maze of narrow streets in the city, Outram had sent Henry Kavanagh, a minor civil servant, who disguised himself as an Indian and, carrying a message to Campbell, passed through the enemy lines. For this brave deed Kavanagh was later to receive a

26. Map of the entrenched position of the British at Lucknow.

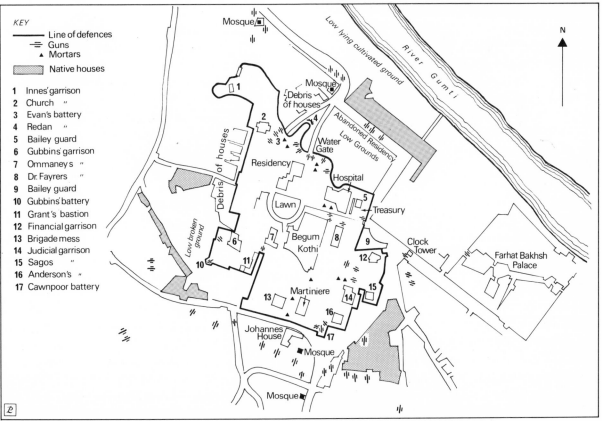

KEY
— Line of defences
⚏ Guns
▲ Mortars
▨ Native houses

1 Innes' garrison
2 Church "
3 Evan's battery
4 Redan "
5 Bailey guard
6 Gubbins' garrison
7 Ommaney's "
8 Dr. Fayrer's "
9 Bailey guard
10 Gubbins' battery
11 Grant's bastion
12 Financial garrison
13 Brigade mess
14 Judicial garrison
15 Sagos "
16 Anderson's "
17 Cawnpoor battery

27. Captain Gough, in typical dress of a British officer of native cavalry during the Mutiny, depicted winning his Victoria Cross at Lucknow.

During 1858 the enemy strongholds at Jhansi, Bareilly and Gwalior fell and soon all the affected regions, except Rajaputana and Central India, were pacified. Tantia Topi, the ex-commander of Nana Sahib's bodyguard, kept up a guerilla campaign in Central India until his betrayal and capture in April 1859.

On 8 July 1859, Lord Canning issued a proclamation which officially declared peace in India. 'War is at an end; Rebellion is put down; the Noise of Arms is no longer heard where the enemies of the State have persisted in their last Struggle; the Presence of large Forces in the Field has ceased to be necessary; Order is re-established; and peaceful Pursuits have everywhere been resumed.' Both Europeans and Indians, aghast at the savagery of both sides, laboured to build a better future.

Chronology

rarely-awarded civilian Victoria Cross.

The final relief of Lucknow was accomplished on 17 November, when Campbell's army fought it's way through to the Residency. Campbell's main concern was not to hold the city, but to evacuate the sick and wounded and the women and children, which was done without difficulty. Leaving Outram and a strong force a few miles from Lucknow, until he could return and drive the rebels from the city, Colin Campbell hurried back to Cawnpore where a rebel force of 20,000 men under Tantia Topi was preparing to attack. Arriving just in time he defeated the rebel army on 6 December and then set about completing the pacification of Oudh. It was not until March 1858 that the city of Lucknow was finally captured by Campbell, but by this time many of the rebels had escaped, some of them joining the Rani of Jhansi who was waging a successful campaign against Sir Hugh Rose in Central India.

With the capture of Delhi and Lucknow, however, the outcome of the Mutiny was settled.

1857

January	Rumour of the greased cartridges at Dum-Dum
February	Mutiny of the 19th Bengal Native Infantry at Berhampur
March	19th Bengal Native Infantry disbanded at Barrackpur
April	Outbreaks of incendiarism at Ambala
May	Disbandment of the 7th Irregular Cavalry at Lucknow
	Disbandment of the 34th Bengal Native Infantry at Barrackpur
	Mutiny and massacre at Meerut followed by outbreak at Delhi, Bombay, Ferozepur, Bareilly and many other stations
	Delhi Field Force reaches Karnaul
	General Anson the British Commander-in-Chief dies
June	Uprisings continue throughout the Bengal Presidency
	Mutiny at Cawnpore followed by the siege of the entrenchment and the massacre of the survivors

28. Kavanagh donning his disguise (note corks being burnt to blacken his face) before leaving besieged Lucknow on the mission which won him the Victoria Cross.

Mutiny at Lucknow and the Europeans take up their position in the Residency

British troops defeated at Chinhat near Lucknow

The siege of Lucknow begins

Battle of Bedli-ke-serai followed by the Delhi Field Force taking up its position on the Ridge and starting siege operations

July   General Barnard, commanding at Delhi, dies

Havelock advances from Allahabad towards Cawnpore. Arrives on 17 July, too late to stop the massacre of the women and children

August   Siege of Lucknow continues

Havelock's first attempt to relieve the beleaguered Residency fails

September Assault and capture of Delhi

Residency at Lucknow relieved by Havelock and Outram

Second siege of Lucknow Residency begins

November Lucknow relieved by Colin Campbell, the new Commander-in-Chief Residency evacuated and city temporarily abandoned

December Tantia Topi's army defeated by Colin Campbell

1858

January   Colin Campbell starts campaign to recapture Lucknow

Hugh Rose begins Central India Campaign

March   Lucknow recaptured by Colin Campbell

April   Tantia Topi defeated at Betwa by Hugh Rose

29. Drum of the 1st Royal Madras Fusiliers, carried during the Relief of Lucknow.

	Storming of Jhansi, the Rani flees
	Jhansi finally captured on 6 April
	Colin Campbell begins pacification of
	Rohilkhand
May	Pacification of Rohilkhand complete
	Guerilla warfare begins
June	Rani of Jhansi and Tantia Topi
	seize Gwalior
	Battle of Kotah-ke-serai, Rani of
	Jhansi killed
	Battle of Gwalior
	Capture of Gwalior and flight of
	Tantia Topi
	Pacification of guerilla forces in Oudh
July	Tantia Topi continues active resis-
	tance in Rajputana and Central
	India
1859	
April	Tantia Topi betrayed and captured
	Trial of Tantia Topi on the 15th
	Tantia Topi executed on 18 April
July	Proclamation officially declaring
	peace in India

The Plates

(Additional research by G. A. Embleton)

A1 Officer, 24th Regiment of Foot (2nd Warwickshire)
A typical officer of 'Queen's troops' in Home Service Dress. The scarlet 1856 tunic is faced in regimental colour at collar and cuffs, and has slashed panels of the same on the cuffs and scarlet ones on the rear skirts. Collar, cuffs cuff-slashes, and leading edge are piped white; there is gold lace round the top and front of the collar, and horizontally round the top of the cuff, and three button loops of the same appear on each slash. The crimson sash of commissioned rank is worn over the left shoulder, where it is retained by a scarlet twist shoulder-cord. The blue trousers with a red welt down the outside are typical of the entire infantry of the line. The shako is the second Albert pattern, of black beaver with glazed leather top and front and rear peaks; the front peak is squared and horizontal, the rear peak a rounded continuation of the shape of the shako body. A white-over-red pompon rises at the front from a gilt metal holder, above a rayed gilt star with the regimental number cut out in the centre, the whole surmounted by a crown. The height of the shako was $5\frac{1}{4}$ inches at the front and 7 inches at the rear; it was introduced in January 1855. The 24th was at Rawalpindi when the Mutiny broke out; it saw action on several occasions, notably at Jhelum, where 300 men of the 1st Bn, with three guns, attacked and drove off 1,000 well-armed mutineers.

A2 Private, 7th Regiment of Foot (Royal Fusiliers)
Typical Other Rank of Queen's infantry in Home Service Dress with forage cap. This latter was of blue cloth with the regimental number or badge on the front in brass – here, the grenade of the fusiliers, with cut-out '7'. The red cloth tunic has the regimental facing colour – here, the blue of all 'Royal' regiments – at collar, cuff, cuff-slash and shoulder straps. The collar is piped white all round; and white piping appears

round the shoulder straps, down the leading edge, round the top of the cuff, and on three sides of the cuff-slashes, as well as round the skirt-slashes. The equipment is the improved 1850 pattern; note the cap-pouch for percussion caps on the crossbelt. The weapon is the three-band Enfield rifle; the 1851 Minié rifle, recognizable by its lack of barrel-bands and its overall superficial resemblance to the old 'Brown Bess', was still used by some Queen's regiments during the Mutiny.

A3 Sowar, Bengal Light Cavalry

This trooper – *sowar* – of native light horse represents the branch in which the spark of Mutiny first flared. The painting is taken from a contemporary drawing by Atkinson, our main source of eye-witness material. The surviving material suggests that the undress uniform illustrated here was in general use as field and daily service dress. It is in 'French grey', faced at collar and pointed cuff with red or orange, and consists of a simple round-bottomed stable jacket and overalls. Both are decorated with white tape, and the overalls have a broad side-stripe; note the piping on the rear sleeve seam. The dark blue forage cap has a white tuft and band. After the outbreak of the Mutiny, rebellious horse and foot alike largely reverted to white native clothing.

B1 British officer, 2nd Punjab Cavalry (Probyn's Horse)

Raised in 1849, this Sikh regiment was usually referred to as Probyn's Horse during the Mutiny, after its commander Captain Dighton Probyn. The Punjabi regiments remained loyal, and saw considerable action; Probyn's riders fought with distinction at Delhi and Lucknow. The regimental coat, the red *alkalak*, was worn richly laced with gold by officers; in cold weather it was normal to cover it with a skin *poshteen* worn hair inside. Light yellowish khaki (*multanimutti*) trousers and high boots were worn. The Indian officers wore gold-laced dark blue turbans, the British officers helmets of dark felt with a dark blue *paggri*; for parade these bore flowing white hair plumes, but in the field a brass spike was substituted. The use of mail gauntlets and even whole mail sleeves, as a protection against sabre cuts, is well attested. The *kamarband* – sash – worn by this officer is a

Kashmiri shawl. A percussion revolver, perhaps a Colt, is carried in addition to the heavy cavalry sabre. This painting is based on a photograph and a reconstruction by C. A. Norman published in *Tradition* magazine. See Plate D2.

It is interesting that the Duke of Wellington suggested that the Honourable East India Company dress their troops in red versions of native dress, rather than the uncomfortable copies of British regular uniform then favoured. It took the desperate improvisations of the Mutiny to underline the common sense in this suggestion, and after the Mutiny the Indian Army adopted the uniforms based on native styles which it made famous for a century thereafter.

B2 Private, 1st Madras Fusiliers

The Company army included regiments of European troops as well as the native regiments which made up its bulk. The Madras Fusiliers were nicknamed 'Neill's Blue-caps', according to the letters of a Naval officer, because they were unable to obtain white covers and neck curtains for their peaked forage caps and so made use of blue. Pictorial evidence suggests that fading and washing produced a variety of shades of blue

---

FACING COLOURS OF
BENGAL NATIVE
INFANTRY REGIMENTS

Yellow 2, 3, 4, 8, 18, 21, 36, 37, 41, 42, 47, 48, 53, 54, 61, 62, 63, 64, 65, 67, 68, 70, 72, 73, 74 *Dark Green* 6, 7, 10, 13, 19, 23, 28, 29, 38, 39, 45, 46, 51, 52 *White* 1, 5, 9, 11, 12, 20, 22, 24, 35, 55, 56, 66, 69 *Buff* 14, 16, 30, 31, 49, 50, 57, 58 *Black* 17, 32, 33, 71 *Blue* 25, 34, 40 *Red* 26, 27 *Pea Green* 43, 44 *Saxon Green* 59, 60 *French Grey* 15

(Of the ten regiments of Bengal Light Cavalry, the 5th BLC wore black facings and all the other regiments, orange.)

including this light tone. The white jacket and red-welted blue trousers seem to have been normal service dress. The figure is taken from a C. A. Norman reconstruction.

B3 British officer
Typical improvised campaigning kit, with a straw 'wide-awake' hat decorated with a veil or *paggri*, and a red shell jacket. The red jackets were usually replaced with white or white dyed khaki in the field.

B4 Private, 1st Bengal Fusiliers
This Company regiment of Europeans were known as the 'Dirtyshirts'; we owe our knowledge of their dress to an Atkinson drawing of 1857 and the memoir of Lieutenant Majendie published in 1861. The white-covered forage cap was sometimes worn with a *paggri* tied round it according to individual taste. The grey shirt, worn outside blue trousers with red welts, made a practical hot-weather campaigning uniform; a black kerchief was loosely knotted at the neck. Standard white infantry equipment was worn. At the relief of Lucknow a blue jacket appears to have been worn. Officers wore drab jackets of loose cut, with the high wicker helmets of Romanesque shape, covered in white cloth and often with a knotted *paggri*, which proved popular during the Mutiny.

B5 Trooper, 9th Lancers
A watercolour by Upton dated 1857 illustrates a short white stable jacket and white trousers, a white-covered forage cap with a removable neck curtain, and standard equipment. The collar, shoulder straps and pointed cuffs are piped in red. This uniform is confirmed by Anson and Atkinson. Although this type of light and practical dress was worn by many units, it is worth noting that some Queen's cavalry, notably the 2nd and 6th Dragoon Guards, suffered agonies through soldiering on in heavy European uniforms and helmets

C1 Havildar, Nasiri Bn. (66th Goorkha Regt., Bengal Native Infantry)
The Gurkha regiments were models of loyalty during the Mutiny, distinguishing themselves in action alongside Queen's troops, and cementing the affectionate ties which are traditional between the 'Tommy' and the 'Johnny Gurkha'. The Nasiri Battalion, formerly the irregular 4th Rifle Battalion, was taken into the Bengal line in 1850 after distinguishing itself in a local mutiny in 1849; it took over the number of the disbanded mutinous regiment. At the outbreak of the Mutiny hasty British precautions prompted by unjustified doubts as to the regiment's reliability caused much ill-feeling; but after the pride of the Gurkhas had been soothed by the tact of one Captain Briggs the regiment returned to its duty and gave no further cause for alarm. The very dark Rifle green uniform traditional among Gurkha units is faced black at collar and cuff. There are black shoulder straps, and green 'wings' laced and tufted with black. The three chevrons of this rank, equivalent to sergeant, appear in black on both upper arms. Equipment is of Rifle pattern, in black leather. This, and the next figure, are taken from a group photograph by Felice Beato.

C2 British officer, Nasiri Bn. (66th Goorkha Regt., B.N.I.)
The 66th was commanded throughout the Mutiny by Alexander Bagot. This figure illustrates the Rifle-style uniform and belts, with the black facings and frogging and silver whistle-fittings traditional to Rifle corps.

C3 Sergeant-Major, British line infantry
On arrival in India Queen's troops were issued with white trousers, white tunics and shell jackets, and white cap covers. This senior NCO wears this white hot-weather uniform with the distinctions of his rank. The crimson sash is worn on the right shoulder, and the four gold lace chevrons, backed red, are surmounted by a crown in heraldic colours.

D1 Sepoy, Rifle Company, 41st Bengal Native Infantry
(This figure, and D3, are painted after the Charles Wyndham print of 1853.) The usual establishment of a BNI regiment was about one thousand men in ten companies. There were 120 native NCOs, and 20 native officers; ten European

30. Elephant Battery siege gun at Lucknow.

company officers, and a European commander, adjutant, quartermaster, and occasionally one or two other staff officers. The 41st had its barracks at Seetanpoor. This soldier of the rifle company wears a uniform clearly inspired by British Rifle styles, in very dark green faced black at collar, cuffs and tufted shoulder straps. The buttons are brass, and black-on-black square button loops appear on the cuffs. Leather equipment is in Rifle style, and the weapon is the old Brunswick rifle first issued in 1838. The Kilmarnock cap became the official headgear of the BNI, replacing the tall shako, in 1847. In summer it

was buttoned into a white cover; it was made of dark blue cloth with a white band – dark green for light troops. Note the regimental number and bugle horn badge in brass on the cover.

D2 Sowar, 2nd Punjab Cavalry

Trooper of Probyn's Horse; cf. the officer, Plate B1. The dark blue turban apart, the uniforms are basically identical, though obviously undecorated for a trooper. The Sikh religion forbade the cutting of hair or facial hair, so fierce beards and moustaches were the norm among Punjabi troops. Note the *tulwar* sabre. At the time of its raising in

31. Charge of the British cavalry at Lucknow.

1849 the second-in-command of this regiment was Lieutenant S. J. Browne – 'Sam' Browne, who gave his name to the well-known military belt.

D3 Sepoy, 41st Regiment, Bengal Native Infantry
The Kilmarnock worn by this battalion-company private bears the regimental number only. The red coatee, with yellow regimental facings and paired loops of square-ended white tape, has short tails with white turn-backs – see Plate G3. Its inspiration by archaic, Napoleonic-period British Line styles is immediately obvious. The trousers are dark blue without red welts. The equipment seems to be a transitional style, comprising both crossbelts and a waist-belt; most drawings of the Mutiny illustrate the use of a waist-belt and a single crossbelt over the left shoulder. The weapon is the Brunswick rifle. On top of the pack is the characteristic brass drinking bowl or *lotah*.

The regiments of the BNI were usually raised in proportions of around 800 Hindus and 200 Mohammedans. Among the Hindus, recruitment crossed caste lines, and men of high, medium and relatively low caste would all be found in one unit. This sometimes had a bad effect on discipline and morale. Promotion from *sepoy* to *naik* (corporal), *havildar* (sergeant), *jemadar* (lieutenant) and *subadar* (captain) was strictly by seniority, and was thus very slow. Senior native ranks were often men in their sixties.

E1 Private, 91st Regiment of Foot (Argyllshire Regiment)
Sent out to India from Corfu in 1858, the 91st were issued '. . . white duck frocks and trousers with covers to forage caps', but by November they were reported as wearing '. . . suits of cotton twill, loose tunics and trousers of a light drab colour' (G. L. Goff, *Historical Records*). The many shades, collectively termed khaki or drab, were obtained by dyeing white duck with a number of different substances each of which produced its own variation: tea, coffee, curry powder and ordinary mud were all pressed into service. Contemporary descriptions reflect this variety, and it is interesting to note how often suggestions of a blue tinge turn up: '. . . puce

colour ...', '... karkee – a sort of bluish slate colour', '... bluish brown called karky ...', '... this karkee ... was a sort of grey drab ...', and so on. Note the quilted neck curtain – a common contemporary feature – and the improvised or privately purchased water bottle. The weapon is the three-band Enfield first issued in 1853.

E2 Officer, British line infantry
This field officer wears typical campaign dress. The forage cap is covered and has a white neck curtain; the chinstrap has been looped up over the crown. The tunic is replaced by the undress shell jacket in scarlet, a single-breasted, round-bottomed garment with collar and pointed three-and-a-half inch high cuffs in the regimental facing colour. Details varied from unit to unit, and some regiments wore white-piped jackets. Ranking appeared on the collar in embroidery – here, a gold crown – and both shoulders bear gold cords. Officers supplied their own firearms; this one carries the excellent and popular five-shot Adams revolver.

E3 Private, 52nd Regiment of Foot (Oxfordshire Light Infantry)
The typical appearance of a soldier of the 52nd during the siege of Delhi. The loose flannel shirt, dyed khaki, was worn outside the red-welted blue trousers, with a sash at the waist. The forage cap had a cover, curtain, and paggri, all of khaki. The equipment was worn over the shirt and sash. This regiment did not receive an issue of the round, blue-painted canteens, and used lemonade bottles in leather covers. A contemporary description states that all ranks wore the same outfit in the Delhi trenches; when wearing the khaki-dyed white tunics NCOs fastened white chevrons to the sleeves with hooks and eyes, and officers were distinguished only by their gilt buttons.

F1 Officer, Hodson's Horse
One of the most famous corps of the Indian Army, this unit originated as a number of separate bodies of cavalry, but in 1857 they were embodied at Delhi under the command of Lieutenant W.S.R. Hodson. The regiment, of loyal Sikhs, attracted considerable attention, often in association with Probyn's Horse; there are several contemporary mentions of their 'wild and bold ... carriage'. Late in 1857 the regiment was issued at Ambala with winter uniforms consisting of dark blue quilted coats with red paggris, kamarbands and kullahs (the cap round which the paggri was wound), and khaki trousers. Our figure is based on material relevant to the earlier period, however, when the regiment wore white summer dress. A print showing the regiment in action at Rhotuck near Delhi illustrates this white single-breasted jacket and white trousers tucked into high black boots, with black belts and pouches. It shows Hodson himself wearing a white-covered wicker helmet, of the locally made type popular with British officers for its coolness and (when wound with many folds of cloth) protection. In the print Hodgson's paggri is yellow; but an eyewitness description by Verney mentions a red paggri, and this is also shown in a portrait – it seems entirely logical, since red was the unit's distinguishing colour. Verney also mentions the Kashmiri scarf worn at the waist.

F2 Captain, Naval Brigade
This painting is taken from a print and a portrait of Captain William Peel at Lucknow. The familiar Romanesque helmet is worn with a neck curtain. Gold lace ranking is worn on the cuffs of the dark blue frock coat. The interesting sword worn by Peel from a black waist-belt was made to his own requirements by Henry Wilkinson, the celebrated swordsmith, after the pattern of a Roman gladius. Some excavations across Peel's family property in 1856, in the path of the Sandy-Potton Railway, had turned up a cache of Roman remains, among them a sword which so impressed Peel that he ordered the copy for his own use!

F3 Officer, Bengal Foot Artillery
The simple hot-weather uniform worn by this officer is taken from a photograph of two such officers at Lucknow. The collar and cuffs are in regimental facing colour, and the forage cap is swathed in a white paggri and has a curtain. The other officer in the photograph has a similar uniform, but with white-on-white braid frogging on the jacket.

32. Lieutenant-Colonel Henry Drury Harness, Royal Engineers (1804–1883), who commanded the engineers in the force under Lord Clyde, and was present at the siege and capture of Lucknow.

G1 Private, 92nd Regiment of Foot (Gordon Highlanders)

The Highland bonnet of black ostrich feathers had six tails hanging down on the right side. The diced band is hidden here by a thickly-quilted sunshade laced in place. A white plume rises from a black cockade with the regimental badge in the centre – this is also hidden here. Note the characteristic Scots cut of the white summer tunic, worn here with the Gordon kilt. The equipment is the improved 1850 pattern.

G2 Trooper, 7th Hussars

A contemporary drawing by Crealock forms the basis for this figure. The light drab jacket fastens at the front in some manner not entirely clear. The peakless forage cap is enveloped in a *paggri* and curtain. The blue overalls are 'booted' at the bottom with leather. Note the slits at the hips of the jacket, and the very low collar. White pouch belts with black pouches and small white cap pouches are believed to have been worn.

G3 Bengal sepoy mutineer

This figure represents the typical appearance of a Bengal sepoy at the time of the outbreak. Sources are contradictory on the equipment – it is possible some sepoys still wore the old style with two crossbelts for bayonet and pouch, rather than the waist-belt with frogged bayonet shown here. The trousers seem to have been the first item of European uniform discarded by the mutineers, who gratefully reverted to their white *dhoti* or loincloth. (This was usually worn beneath the trousers, and was the normal working dress.) There seems to be no particular consensus on the dress worn by sepoys later in the Mutiny: some discarded uniform entirely and wore the *dhoti* with a white shirt opening down one side of the chest, and a white skull-cap or loose *paggri*, while isolated groups seem to have retained the trappings of their Company service even down to colours and the regimental band. The majority of eyewitness accounts speak of white clothing. The weapon of the BNI was in most cases a smoothbore percussion musket of obsolete pattern.

H1 Officer, 93rd Regiment of Foot (Sutherland Highlanders)

A favourite regiment of Sir Colin Campbell's, the Sutherland Highlanders were equally devoted to him, and greatly distinguished themselves in the recapture of Lucknow at the Sikanderbargh and Shah Najaf gates. Sir Colin led them into action himself at the latter obstacle – probably the last time in history that a Commander-in-Chief rode into battle, sword in hand, among the pipers of his leading infantry. In 24 hours the 93rd won seven Victoria Crosses, and the epic ended with a twelve-year-old piper defiantly playing 'Cock 'o the North' at the foot of the tattered Colours, planted under fire on the tower of the Shah Najaf.

The 14-inch black ostrich feather bonnet had a diced band and a white vulture feather plume rising from a black cockade bearing the regimental badge (see H2). The officers' tunic was of pale khaki alpaca with red facings and two red twist shoulder-cords. The broadsword was suspended from a crossbelt with a regimental plate, and the crimson net sash of commissioned rank was worn over the left shoulder. The kilt of Sutherland tartan was set off, for officers and senior NCOs, by a sporran displaying the mask of a badger. Note the elaborate officer's dirk, with two smaller knives sheathed on the face of the silver-mounted scabbard.

H2 Private, 93rd Regiment of Foot (Sutherland Highlanders)

The uniform, described and sketched by Collier and Crealock, was intended for use in China; the regiment was diverted to India in the emergency. For rank and file the khaki jacket was of Holland cloth with shoulder straps – note the regimental number in brass. Greatcoats were sometimes worn rolled bandolier-fashion. The bonnet cockade and badge is clearly visible here; it is reported that the lining was removed in some cases, for lightness and coolness. The sporran did not display the badger's mask of the more elaborate pattern.

H3 Private, 95th Regiment of Foot (Derbyshire)

The regiment took the number of the old 95th Rifle Regiment, removed from the line in 1816. It earned the nickname 'the Nails' in the Crimea, for being 'hard as nails'; and in the Mutiny fought several engagements including Awah and Kotah, at the second of which Private McQuirt won the regiment's first V.C. It is also recorded that at Kotah the regiment adopted a ram as a mascot, naming it 'Derby'; this intrepid beast marched with the 95th over some 3,000 miles of Indian roads, and at the end of the campaign was awarded the Mutiny Medal – a decoration still worn by his successors on parade!

The dark blue peaked forage cap has a white cover and curtain. The usual blue trousers with red welts, and 1850 equipment, are worn here with a red shell jacket faced with the regimental colour at collar, shoulder straps and cuffs and closed by ten regimental buttons.

Légendes

1 Lord Canning – Gouverneur Général des Indes pendant la Révolte des Cipayes. **2** Bahadur Shah – dernier Empereur Mogol des Indes. **3** Cartouche d'un fusil Enfield environ 1857. **4** Sous-Officier du 9e Bengal Cavalerie irrégulière 1852. **5** Conductor Buckley qui aida les Lieutenants Forrest et Willoughby à faire exploser le dépot de munitions à Delhi lorsque les insurgés aient failli le prendre. **6** Des troupes britanniques en route vers Delhi, en tenue de campagne typique. **7** Troupement d'assaut de Fusiliers ramenant un canon au camp britannique sur la crête de Delhi. **8** Cavalier dévoué de Hodson's Horse, 1857. **9** Lieutenant Meecham et Chirugien Anderson avec des cavaliers Sikh dévoués; notez la tenue typique des soldats indigènes et des officiers britanniques. **10** La colonne du canon de siège s'approche de Delhi.

11 Poste de sentinelle des britanniques à Delhi; l'insigne d'une grenade sur leurs boucles identifie les Fusiliers. **12** Des insurgés; la plupart revinrent à la tenue indigène pendant la Révolte. **13** Assaut de la Porte Kashmir à Delhi, le 14 septembre 1857. **14** La Porte Kashmir, Delhi. **15** Des officiers regardent l'attaque sur la Porte Kashmir. **16** Combat dans les rues à Delhi entre les britanniques, l'Infanterie Indienne et les insurgés. Observez l'officier en train d'enclouer un canon. **17** Lieutenant-Colonel Greathead commanda la 9e Infanterie britannique à Delhi. **18** Thomas Ray en uniforme typique de l'époque, avec un accessoire macabre! **19** Elèves de l'école de la Compagnie des Indes à Addiscombe, Surrey, England. **20** Sir James Outram prit la commande à la province d'Oudh en 1857-58.

21 La caserne endommagée par des obus au retranchement de Wheeler à Cawnpore. **22** Le massacre à Cawnpore. L'artiste s'est trompé en montrant l'embuscade des bateaux réfugiés, le massacre des femmes et enfants, et le lancement des cadavres dans le puits dans la même scène; les femmes et les enfants furent tués au moins 15 jours avant l'épisode des bateaux. **23** La résidence à Lucknow. **24** La Martinière, Lucknow; construite par un général français employé par un prince régional au 18e siècle, elle fut fortifiée et défendue par les insurgés pendant l'attaque de Campbell sur la ville. **25** Major General Mansfield et Sir Colin Campbell (à droite), le Commandant en Chef aux Indes pendant la Révolte. Campbell, un commandant doué et bien-aimé de ces hommes, fit l'expérience du combat pour la première fois en 1808 au Portugal, et combattit aussi en Chine, aux Indes et en Crimée. **26** La position entranchée des britanniques à Lucknow. **27** Captain Gough gagnant sa Croix de Victoria à Lucknow; il porte la tenue typique d'un officier britannique de la Cavalerie indigène. **28** Kavanagh déguisé, il a son visage noirci avec du liège brûlé avant de s'échapper de Lucknow chercher du secours. **29** Le tambour des 1er Fusiliers Royal Madras, porté à la relève de Lucknow. **30** Un canon du siège tiré par un éléphant à Lucknow. **31** La charge de la Cavalerie britannique à Lucknow. **32** Lieutenant-Colonel Harness commanda les Royal Engineers à Lucknow.

Planches en couleurs

A1 Officier, 24e Infanterie (2e Warwickshire Regt.) en Home Service Dress. La tunique 1856 est portée avec des parements verts, la couleur du régiment. Le shako est le 'deuxième modèle Albert' de 1855. On reconnaît les officiers par l'écharpe écarlate. **A2** Simple soldat, 7e Infanterie (Royal Fusiliers) en Home Service Dress avec un calot. Le fusil est un 'Enfield', et l'équipement en cuir est du modèle 'amélioré de 1850'. **A3** Cavalier de la Cavalerie legère Bengalèse, en uniforme 'gris français' avec des parements oranges et passepoil blanc. Ceci est la partie de l'armée où la Révolte a éclaté en premier.

B1 Un officier britannique de la 2e Cavalerie Punjab (Probyn's Horse) dans une tenue de Cavalerie indigène richement parée, avec un casque en feutre à la place du turban porté par les cavaliers et officiers indiens. Des gants en cotte de mailles étaient portés pour se protéger contre les coupures d'épée. Observez un des premiers revolvers Colt à la ceinture. Les régiments dévoués de Sikh se battirent avec éclat dans beaucoup de batailles de la Révolte des Cipayes. **B2** Simple soldat des 1er Fusiliers Madras, un régiment d'européens soulevé par la Compagnie des Indes. **B3** Une tenue typique d'un officier d'Infanterie, avec un chapeau de paille et un blouson court. **B4** Simple soldat, 1er Bengal Fusiliers – un autre régiment européen de l'Armée de la Compagnie. L'usage de longues jupes portées à l'extérieur des pantalons comme tenue de campagne par temps chaud était répandu aux Indes; ainsi que l'usage du calot recouvert d'une tissues blanc ou brun écru, et un collet sur le cou. **B5** Cavalier, 9e Lanciers; cet uniforme blanc avec passepoil rouge au col, aux poignets et épaules, est tiré des esquisses de l'époque. Certains cavaliers britanniques portèrent toujours des casques lourds et des uniformes européens et souffrirent terriblement de la chaleur.

C1, C2 Un Sous-Officier et un officier britannique du Bataillon Nasiri de l'Infanterie Gourkha. Ces troupes dévoués Népâlais portèrent des uniformes modelés sur ceux des régiments britanniques d'Infanterie légère, en vert agrémenté de noir. Leur courage et dévouement pendant la Révolte menèrent à une affection intime et durable entre les troupes britanniques et gourkhas qui existe toujours. **C3** Un adjudant-chef, infanterie britannique, par temps chaud en uniforme blanc avec la ceinture et un insigne au bras d'un Sergeant-Major.

39

D1 Simple soldat d'une compagnie de voltigeurs, 41st Bengal Native Infantry. Les Compagnies du Centre portèrent des tuniques rouges; le voltigeur porte le vert et noir des régiments britanniques d'infanterie légère. **D2** Cavalier de la 2e Cavalerie Punjab – comparez-le avec l'officier dans l'image B1. **D3** Simple soldat d'une Compagnie du Centre, 41st Bengal Native Infantry. Cet uniforme est d'un modèle démodé, ressemblant aux modèles britanniques de l'époque napoléonienne. Le fusil Brunswick est porté par ces deux soldats d'infanterie.

E1 Simple soldat 91e Infanterie (Argyllshire). Des vêtements blancs d'été furent teints en khaki atténué ou gris avec des matériaux régionaux et une grande variété de couleurs en résulta. **E2** Officier d'infanterie britannique en blouson court, calot recouvert et pantalons blancs. Il porte un révolver Adams. Des parements de la couleur du régiment décorent le col et les poignets, et l'insigne du rang – ici c'est la couronne d'un commandant – est porté sur le col. **E3** Ce soldat de la 52e infanterie pendant le siège de Delhi porte une autre tenue typique de campagne, un calot recouvert, chemise et pantalons roulés.

F1 Cette image montre Lieutenant Hodson, commandeur de Hodson's Horse, une unité de Cavalerie Sikh dévouée. Son casque est d'osier entouré de tissus – étant frais et offrant une certaine protection contre les coups d'épée. Un turban rouge était signe distinctif du régiment. **F2** Captain, Royal Navy, d'après un portrait du Captain William Peel. Il porte une épée achetée personnellement et fabriquée spécialement en imitation d'un glaive romain. Peel combattit à Lucknow avec la Brigade Navale. **F3**. Uniforme simple de temps chaud, d'après une photo de deux officiers de cet unité à Lucknow.

G1 Ce Highlander de la 91e Infanterie porte un kilt du tartan du clan Gordon et une veste blanche d'été d'une coupe caractéristique des écossais. Un pare-soleil piqué est attaché à la coiffure à plumes d'autruche. **G2** Cavalier des 7e Hussars dont l'uniforme dessiné par un témoin oculaire; le calot est caché dans les plis du paggri (turban), et les pantalons sont agrémentés de 'fausses bottes' en cuir. **G3** Un insurgé Sepoy de Bengale, dans son uniforme réglementaire, mais ayant laissé de côté les pantalons pour des bandes-culottes traditionnelles très appréciées des troupes indigènes. La plupart revinrent entièrement aux vêtements blancs indigènes – voir photo 12.

H1, H2 Officier et soldat du 93e Infanterie (Sutherland Highlanders) dans des blousons khakis fournis à l'origine pour le service en Chine avant la diversion de l'unité vers les Indes. Observez le sporran travaillé de l'officier, avec une tête de blaireau, et le beau poignard en ébène et argent. La coiffure du soldat déploie la bande quadrillée, la cocarde noire, insigne du régiment et plumet. Ce régiment s'est beaucoup distingué à Lucknow, où Sir Colin Campbell lui-même le conduit à l'attaque. **H3** Soldat du 95e Infanterie (Derbyshire) en tunique courte et rouge parée de la couleur du régiment. Ces 'shell jackets' remplacèrent fréquemment les tuniques à longues jupes Home Service pour les officiers et les soldats.

Überschrift

1 Lord Canning, General Gouvernor Indiens während der Sepoy-Meuterei. **2** Bahadur Shah, letzte Mogul-Kaiser Indiens. **3** Patrone eines Enfield Gewehrs, c.1857. **4** Unteroffizier, 9th Bengal Irregular Cavalry, 1852. **5** Conductor Buckley, zusammen mit Lieutenants Forrest und Willoughby half er die Delhi Munitionsmagazin, kurz bevor er aus den Rebellen erobert wurde, in die Luft jagen. **6** Britische Truppen auf dem Marsch nach Delhi in typischer Felduniform. **7** Eine Überfallgruppe der Fusiliers kehren mit einer eroberten Kanone ins britische Lager auf einem Höhenzug zurück. **8** Treue Gemeiner, Hodson's Horse, 1857. **9** Lieutenant Meecham und Surgeon Anderson mit treue Sikh Reiter. Diese typischen Uniformen der eingeborenen Soldaten und britische Offiziere sind zu beachten. **10** Die Belagerungsgeschützcolonne nähert sich Delhi.

11 Britische Wachposten, Delhi. Das Granatenemblem an den Schnallen deutet an den Fusiliers hin. **12** Rebellen. Die meisten trugen ihre einheimischen Trachten während der Meuterei. **13** Sturm auf das Kaschmir-Tor, Delhi, 14.September 1857. **14** Kaschmir-Tor, Delhi. **15** Offiziere schauen den Angriff auf das Kaschmir-Tor zu. **16** Strassenkampf zwischen britische und indische Infanterie und den aufständischen Kriegern in Delhi. Zu beachten ist der Offizier, der einem Nagel ins Feuerloch einer Kanone hämmert. **17** Lieutenant-Colonel Greathead, Chef der britischen 9th Regt. of Foot in Delhi. **18** Thomas Ray, in der für die Periode typische Tropenuniform (mit grauenhaften Zubehöre!) **19** Kadetten der Ostindien Gesellschaft-Kadettenanstalt in Addiscombe, England. **20** Sir James Outram, Kommissar und Oberbefehlshaber im Provinz Oudh, 1857–58.

21 Artillerie-beschädigte Kaserne innerhalb Wheelers-Schwanze, Cawnpore. **22** Der Massenmord zu Cawnpore. Der Kunstler hat einem Fehler begangen indem er den Überfall der Flüchtlingsboote, das Töten Frauen und Kinder und das neineinwerfen Toter in einen Brunnen alles zusammen gebracht hat. Das Mördern der Frauen und Kinder fand in der Tat über zwei Wochen nach dem Bootsüberfall statt. **23** Die Residenz, Lucknow. **24** La Martiniere, Lucknow. Wurde in 18. Jahrhundert von einem französischen General auf Befehl des regierenden Fürsten erbaut un während Campbells Angriff auf die Stadt von den Rebellen befestigt und verteidigt. **25** Major-General Mansfield, und General Sir Colin Campbell (Rechts), Oberbefehlshabers Indiens während der Meuterei. Campbell, ein begabte und beliebte Befehlshaber, erführ 1808 in Portugal seine Feuertaufe. Er kämpfte spater in China, Indien und in Krimkrieg. **26** Die verschanzte britische Stellung, Lucknow. **27** Captain Gough verdiente sein Victoria Cross in Lucknow. Seine Uniform ist für britische Offiziere der eingeborenen Kavallerie-Regimentern typisch. **28** Kavanagh, verkleidet und mit seinem Gesicht mit Korkenschwarz getarnt,

kurz bevor er aus Lucknow um Hilfe herbeizubringen wegschlich. **29** Trommel des 1st Royal Madras Fusiliers. Sie wurde beim Entsatz von Lucknow geschlagen. **30** Belagerungsgeschütz, von Elefanten gezogen, bei Lucknow. **31** Britische Kavallerieangriff bei Lucknow. **32** Lieutenant-Colonel Harness, Befehlshaber der Royal Engineers in Lucknow.

Farbtafeln

A1 Offizier, 24th Foot (2nd Warwickshire Regt.) in der 'Home Service Dress' Uniform. Der Rock M1856 zeigt die grüne Abzeichenfarbe. Der Shako M1855 hiess auch 'Zweite Albert Müster'. Die dunkelrote Schärpe ist Zeichen der Offiziers würde. **A2** Gemeiner, 7th Foot (Royal Fusiliers) in der 'Home Service Dress' mit Feldmütze. Das Gewehr ist ein Enfield, das Lederzeug die sog. 'M1850 Verbesserte Ausführung'. **A3** Gemeiner, Bengal Light Cavalry in 'französisch-grauer' Uniform mit orangefarbigen Abzeichen und weissem Tressenbesatz. In dieser Waffengattung brach die Meuterei zuerst aus.

B1 Britische Offizier des 2nd Punjab Cavalry (Probyn's Horse). Er trägt die reichsbesetzter Ausführung der eingeborenen Kavallerie-Tracht mit Filzhelm statt des Turbans, dass von den Gemeinern und von den indischen Offizieren getragen wurde. Die kettengepanzerten Handschuhe schützte gegen Säbelhiebe. Die Frühausführung des Colt-Revolvers in der schärpe beachten! Die treuen Sikh-Regimenter kämpfte mit Auszeichnung in vielen Schlachten während der Meuterei. **B2** Gemeiner, 1st Madras Fusiliers, eines der europäischen Regimenter der Armee der Gesellschaft. Es war in Indien üblich die langen Hemde über die Hosen im Sommer Feldzug zu tragen. Die Feldmütze ist weissen oder blauen Stoffüberzug mit Nackenschütz war auch oft zu sehen. **B3** Gemeiner, 9th Lancers. Diese weisse Uniform mit roten Vorstoss zu den Kragen, Aufschläge und Schultern wurde einer zeitgenossen Darstellung entnommen. Einige britische Kavallerie-Regimenter trugen immer noch ihre europäische Uniformen unde schwere Helme und hatten viel unter der Hitze zu leiden.

C1 & C2 Unteroffizier und britische Offizier des Nasiri Battalion der Gurkha Infanterie. Diese treue, nepalesische Truppen trugen Uniformen nach britischen Jäger-Regimentern-Art d.h. grün mit schwarz. Ihr Mut und Treue während der Meuterei führte zu einer engen Kameradschaft zwischen britischen und gurkha Truppen, die Heute noch stark ist. **C3** Unteroffizier mit Portepee, britische Infanterie, in weisser Tropenuniform mit Schärpe und Dienstgradabzeichen eines Sergeant-Majors.

D1 Gemeiner, Jägerkompanie, 41st Bengal Native Infantry (41. bengal-Eingeborenen-Infanterie-Regiment). Die Füsilier-Kompanien trugen röte Röcke, die Jägerkompanie dagegen, die grün und schwarz der britischen Jäger-Regimentern. **D2** Gemeiner, 2nd Punjab Cavalry. Vergleich mit dem Offizier auf Tafel B1. **D3** Füsilier-Kompanie, 41st BNI. Die Uniform ist sehr altmodisch und ähnlich wie die britischen Uniformen der napoleonischen Epoche. Die beiden Gemeine tragen das 'Brunswick' gezogene Gewehr.

E1 Gemeiner, 91st Foot (Argyllshire Regiment). Die weisse Tropenuniformen wurden hell-khaki oder grau an Ort und Stelle gefärbt, deswegen kamen häufige Farbenungleichheiten vor. **E2** Offizier (Major) der britischen Infanterie in kurzer Jacke, überzogener Feldmütze und weissen Hosen. Er trägt einem Adams-Revolver. Die Regimentsabzeichenfarbe erscheint auf Kragen und Aufschläge. Das Dienstgradabzeichen – hier eine Krone – wird auf dem Kragen getragen. **E3** Soldat des 52nd Foot während der Delhi-Belagerung. Er trägt eine typische Felduniform mit Hemd, aufgekrempelten Hosen und überzogener Mütze.

F1 Eine Darstellung von Lieutenant Hodson, Chef von Hodson's Horse, eine treue Sikh Kavallerieeinheit. Diese Helme wurde aus Weidenruthen gemacht und mit Tuch überzogen. Er leistete einige Schütz gegen Säbelhiebe und auch gegen die Hitze der Sonne. Der rote Turban war das Regimentsabzeichen. **F2** Captain, Royal Navy. Nach dem Portrait von Captain William Peel. Sein Degen war eine persönliche Einführung, eine Nachahmung des römischen Gladius. Peel kämpfte bei Lucknow mit der Marine-Brigade. **F3** Einfache Tropenuniform, nach eine Aufnahme zwei Offiziere dieser Einheit bei Lucknow.

G1 Dieser Highlander des 92nd Foot trägt einen Schottrock in dem Gordon clan 'Tartan' und weisse Sommerjacke im schottischen Schnitt. Eine wattierte Nackenschütz mit der Strausssfedern besetzten Kopfbedeckung angebunden worden. **G2** Gemeiner, 7th Hussars, nach dem Leben gezeichnet. Die Feldmütze ist unter den 'paggri' (Turban) kaum zu sehen. Die Hosen sind mit ledernen 'falsche Stiefeln' besetzt. **G3** Bengalische Sepoy aufständischer Soldat. Er trägt seine Uniformrock aber statt Hosen hat er sein Lendentuch, dass unter den Inder sehr beliebt war, angelegt. Die Mehrzahl der Rebellen trugen ihre eigene weisse Nationaltracht wie auf der Aufnahme 12 zu sehen ist.

H1 & H2 Offizier und Soldat des 93rd Foot (Sutherland Highlanders). Die braune Jacken wurden ursprünglich für den Dienst in China herausgegeben; das Regiment wurde aber nach Indien umgeleitet. Die komplizierte Beschlag der Felltasche des Offiziers mit der Dachskopfverzierung, und sein Dolch aus Ebenholz und silber beachten. Die Mütze des Soldaten zeigt gewürfeltem Prüfstück, schwarze Nationale, Regimentswappen und Federbusch. Das Regiment hat sich bei Lucknow, wo es unter persönlicher Führung von Sir Colin Campbell in die Schlacht ging, hervorgetan. **H3** Soldat, 95th Foot (Derbyshire Regiment). Die kurze rote Jacke zeigt die Regimentsabzeichenfarbe. Diese 'Shell Jackets' wurden oft statt die 'Home Service Jacken (mit den langen Schossen) von den Offizieren und Mannschaften getragen.